best of
Bill

best of Bill

THE ULTIMATE COLLECTION OF BILL GRANGER'S RECIPES

MURDOCH BOOKS

contents

introduction

I come from a family of butchers and bakers so it's fair to say that food, in some shape or form, was always going to be my destiny. Food is what gives my life rhythm. From healthy family breakfasts, to special Saturday night dinners for friends, or seeing my daughters' faces light up when I take a tray of cookies out of the oven, my week revolves around the endless pleasures of good food.

Some days I cook for pleasure and some days for fuel. In today's world we are bombarded with so much of everything when what we really need is very simple — our health and time to enjoy our friends, loved ones and ourselves. Food anchors all the parts of my life. What I cook each day is dependent on many different factors: time, energy levels, what's in the shops.

On holiday in Paris, I had the luxury of shopping daily at local markets, buying some of the most beautiful produce I've ever seen — blueberries with flavour, pink and white radishes the size of my little finger, just-picked herbs and salad greens, amazing cheeses that just oozed — really extraordinary. While I'd love to be able to shop and cook like this every day, it's not realistic given my increasingly busy life. Sometimes there's barely enough time for a quick trip to the supermarket, but I never let this become a barrier to cooking, or let the job of preparing dinner every day become tedious.

The meal I prepare on a Monday night is different to the celebration lunch I make for friends, but all my food is similarly pared back. The greatest sophistication is in simplicity, and the ability to create good food is one of life's most reassuring skills and is immensely satisfying. I hope these recipes inspire you.

breakfast

Early morning is my favourite time of day, always has been. I love waking up early and pottering in the kitchen while it's still dark outside ... there's something very comforting and nurturing about it.

I'm always amazed at people who don't eat breakfast. I love breakfasts — maybe that's why my restaurants have become well known for them. As far as I can see, if you eat a good breakfast you've done a third of your day's work for eating well. It's pretty simple logic.

I make an effort to have breakfast with my family. We usually all decide on our breakfast, whether it be buckwheat pancakes or soft-boiled eggs or whatever, and we all share in its preparation while getting ready for the day. I can't wait until my girls are old enough to bring me breakfast in bed, but until that time comes we usually have a gang of friends over on a Sunday morning.

As long as it's fresh, it doesn't matter what you serve. Relax, just pop the food and a big jug of juice in the middle of the table and let people help themselves. Remember, you are not a restaurant — and it's about the company after all!

buttermilk pancakes

250 g (9 oz/2 cups) plain (all-purpose) flour
3 teaspoons baking powder
a pinch of salt
2 tablespoons sugar
2 eggs, lightly beaten
750 ml (26 fl oz/3 cups) buttermilk
75 g (2½ oz) unsalted butter, melted
unsalted butter, extra, for greasing the pan

to serve
caramelised plums (see below)
maple syrup
yoghurt

Stir the flour, baking powder, salt and sugar together in a bowl. Add the egg, buttermilk and melted butter and whisk to combine.

Heat a large non-stick frying pan over a medium heat and brush a small portion of butter over the base. For each pancake, ladle 80 ml (2½ fl oz/⅓ cup) of batter into the pan and cook for about 2 minutes, until bubbles appear on the surface. Turn the pancakes over and cook for another minute. Transfer to a plate and keep warm while cooking the rest of the pancakes.

Serve the pancakes in stacks with the plums, a jug of maple syrup and some yoghurt.

To caramelise plums, heat a frying pan over a high heat, cut the plums in half and remove the stones, sprinkle the cut sides with sugar and put the plums in the hot frying pan with the cut side down. Sear the plums until the sugar melts and caramelises. This should take about a minute.

mushrooms on toast

SERVES 4

40 g (1½ oz) unsalted butter, chilled and cubed
1 tablespoon olive oil, plus extra, for brushing
2 garlic cloves, finely chopped
500 g (1 lb 2 oz) mixed small mushrooms, such as button and Swiss brown, halved
sea salt
freshly ground black pepper
1 teaspoon balsamic vinegar
2 tablespoons chopped fresh flat-leaf (Italian) parsley
1 teaspoon chopped fresh tarragon
1 teaspoon grated lemon zest
4 slices sourdough bread
1 garlic clove, extra, for rubbing on bread
250 g (9 oz/1 cup) ricotta cheese

Put half the butter with the oil and chopped garlic in a saucepan over a medium to high heat. Add the mushrooms, 60 ml (2 fl oz/¼ cup) water and salt and pepper, to taste. Cover and cook, stirring occasionally, for about 15 minutes, or until the mushrooms are cooked and the liquid is syrupy. Stir in the balsamic vinegar, parsley, tarragon and lemon zest. Taste for seasoning and adjust if necessary. Whisk the remaining cold butter through to thicken the mushroom sauce.

Brush the bread on both sides with the extra olive oil. Grill (broil) until golden on both sides, cut the extra garlic clove, then rub both sides of the bread with the garlic and place on serving plates. Top with ricotta cheese and then mushrooms and serve immediately.

Mushrooms keep best if you store them in a brown paper bag to allow them to breathe. Keeping them in plastic causes them to sweat.

french toast with fresh berry sauce

SERVES 4

3 eggs
185 ml (6 fl oz/¾ cup) milk
8 thick slices brioche or panettone
30 g (1 oz) unsalted butter

to serve
fresh berry sauce (see below)
icing (confectioners') sugar, for sprinkling

Whisk the eggs and milk together in a bowl to combine. Place the brioche or panettone in a shallow dish and pour the milk mixture over the top. Allow the milk to soak in thoroughly, then turn the bread over and soak the other side — if you are using panettone it will need to be soaked for a little longer because it is drier.

Heat a large non-stick frying pan over a medium to high heat and melt half of the butter. Add four slices of bread to the pan and fry for about 1 minute, until golden. Turn over and cook until the other side is golden. Repeat with the remaining butter and bread.

Serve immediately with the berry sauce, remaining berries and a sprinkling of icing sugar.

FRESH BERRY SAUCE

250 g (9 oz/2 cups) raspberries or mixed berries
60 g (2¼ oz/¼ cup) caster (superfine) sugar
1 tablespoon lemon juice

Put half the berries in a blender with the sugar and lemon juice. Purée until smooth, then pour into a bowl.

bircher muesli with pear and blueberries

200 g (7 oz/2 cups) mixed rolled oats,
barley and rye, or rolled oats
375 ml (1 fl oz/1½ cups) pear juice
2 pears, skin left on and grated
125 g (4½ oz/½ cup) plain yoghurt
4 tablespoons toasted chopped almonds
80 g (2¾ oz/½ cup) blueberries

Put the rolled oats, barley and rye in a bowl with the pear juice and leave to soak for 1 hour, or overnight, in the refrigerator. Add the grated pear and yoghurt and mix well. Spoon the muesli into serving bowls and top each with the toasted almonds and blueberries.

The quickest and easiest way to toast nuts is to dry-fry them in a frying pan over a medium heat. However, don't walk away from them because they burn very quickly.

bill's eggs

FRIED

2 teaspoons olive oil
2 eggs, at room temperature
sea salt
freshly ground black pepper

Place a large non-stick frying pan over a medium to high heat for 1 minute. Add the olive oil and swirl until the base of the pan is evenly coated. Carefully crack the eggs into the pan and sprinkle with salt and pepper. Cook for 1 minute. If you like the yolks of your eggs harder, cover the pan with a lid and cook for another minute. Serve with sourdough or wholemeal toast and spicy tomato relish (see page 47).

SCRAMBLED

2 eggs, at room temperature
80 ml (2½ fl oz/⅓ cup) cream
a pinch of salt
10 g (¼ oz) butter

Place the eggs, cream and salt in a bowl and whisk together. Put the butter in a non-stick frying pan over a high heat. Once the butter is melted, pour in the egg mixture and cook for 20 seconds, or until it begins to set around the edge. Using a wooden spoon, stir and bring the egg mixture on the edge of the pan into the centre. It is important to fold the eggs, not scramble them. Leave for 20 seconds, then repeat the folding process. When the eggs are just set, turn out onto a plate and serve with sourdough or wholemeal toast.

BOILED

Place a saucepan of water over a high heat and bring to the boil. Gently place your eggs, which should be at room temperature, into the water then adjust the heat until the water is simmering. For a soft-boiled egg, cook for 4 minutes, medium-boiled 5–6 minutes and hard-boiled 10 minutes.

POACHED

Fill a shallow frying pan with water until it is 5 cm (2 inches) deep and place over a high heat. Once the water boils, turn off the heat and break the eggs directly into the water. Crack the shells open at the water surface so the eggs simply slide into the water. Cover with a tight-fitting lid and leave to cook for 3 minutes, or until the egg whites are opaque. Remove from the pan with a slotted spoon and drain on a clean tea towel (dish towel).

fresh baked beans

1 tablespoon olive oil
1 onion, finely chopped
100 g (3½ oz) pancetta, chopped
1 garlic clove, crushed
2 anchovies, chopped
1 teaspoon fresh thyme leaves, finely chopped
½ teaspoon dried oregano
400 g (14 oz) tin chopped tomaotes
2 x 400 g (14 oz) tin cannellini beans, rinsed
sea salt
freshly ground black pepper

Preheat the oven to 160°C (315°F/Gas 2–3). Heat the olive oil in a large flameproof casserole dish over a medium heat. Add the onion and cook, stirring for 5–6 minutes until the onion is soft. Add the pancetta and cook, stirring occasionally, for 5 minutes, or until slightly crisp. Add the garlic, anchovies, thyme and oregano and cook, stirring, for another minute.

Add the tomatoes and 125 ml (4 fl oz/½ cup) of water, bring to the boil and then reduce the heat to simmer for 10 minutes. Stir in the beans, put a lid on the casserole dish and bake in the oven for 30 minutes. Season with salt and pepper.

baked eggs with spinach and parmesan

1 tablespoon olive oil
200 g (7 oz) baby spinach leaves
sea salt
freshly ground black pepper
8 eggs
4 tablespoons cream
4 tablespoons grated parmesan cheese

to serve
toast

Preheat the oven to 200°C (400°F/Gas 6). Lightly grease four 9 cm (3½ inch) ramekins (dariole moulds) and place on a baking tray.

Heat a saucepan or frying pan over a medium heat. Add the oil to the pan, then add the spinach and season with salt and pepper. Cook until the leaves are just softened. Drain the spinach in a colander and, as soon as it's cool enough to handle, squeeze out the excess liquid.

Spoon the spinach into the ramekins and break 2 eggs into each ramekin on top of the spinach.

Pour 1 tablespoon of cream over each serving of the eggs and sprinkle with 1 tablespoon of parmesan. Bake for 15 minutes, or until the eggs are set and puffed up. Season and serve immediately with toast.

blueberry and almond toasted muesli

SERVES 4

300 g (10½ oz/3 cups) rolled (porridge) oats

125 ml (4 fl oz/½ cup) apple juice

2 tablespoons vegetable oil

80 g (2¾ oz/½ cup) raw almonds

125 g (4½ oz/1 cup) sunflower seeds

40 g (1½ oz ¼ cup) pepitas (pumpkin seeds)

40 g (1½ oz/¼ cup) sesame seeds

30 g (1 oz/½ cup) flaked coconut

125 g (4½ oz/1 cup) dried blueberries (if you can't get these, use currants or sultanas or a mixture of both)

to serve

raspberry swirl yoghurt (see below)

nectarines, stoned and cut into wedges

milk

Preheat the oven to 160°C (315°F/Gas 2–3). Place all the ingredients, except for the dried blueberries, in a large bowl and stir well to combine. Spread the mixture evenly over a large baking tray and place in the oven for 30 minutes, stirring occasionally until lightly browned.

Remove from the oven, allow to cool then add the blueberries. This muesli can be stored in an airtight container for up to 1 month. Serve with the raspberry swirl yoghurt, nectarines and milk.

To make raspberry swirl yoghurt, just mash ½ cup of raspberries with a fork and lightly ripple through a cup of plain yoghurt.

five-grain porridge with brown sugar peaches

SERVES 4

250 g (9 oz/2½ cups) of mixed grains such
as rolled (porridge) oats, rolled rice,
rolled barley, triticale or kibbled rye
(some health food shops sell a
five-grain mix which I think is ideal)
600 ml (21 fl oz/2½ cups) boiling water
600 ml (21 fl oz/2½ cups) milk
3 peaches, quartered
80 g (2¾ oz/⅓ cup) soft brown sugar

to serve
brown sugar, extra
warmed milk

Preheat the oven to 200°C (400°F/Gas 6). Place the grains and boiling water in a saucepan and stir to combine. Leave for 10 minutes. Add the milk and stir again. Place over a medium heat and slowly bring to the boil. Reduce the heat and simmer for 10 minutes, stirring often.

Meanwhile, place the peaches on a baking tray and sprinkle with the brown sugar. Bake in the oven for about 15 minutes, or until the fruit has softened and slightly caramelised.

Spoon the porridge into serving bowls and top with the peaches. Serve with brown sugar and a jug of warmed milk.

When fresh peaches are out of season you can use dried peaches or other dried fruit by soaking them in boiling water for 5 minutes. Make up more than you need of the grain mix and store in an airtight container for up to 2 months.

ham and gruyère french toast

4 eggs

185 ml (6 fl oz/¾ cup) milk

sea salt

freshly ground black pepper

4 slices white bread, 3 cm (1¼ inch) thick

2 teaspoons dijon mustard

4 slices leg ham, trimmed to fit bread

4 slices gruyère cheese, trimmed to fit bread

1 tablespoon olive oil

Preheat the oven to 180°C (350°F/Gas 4). Place the eggs, milk, salt and pepper into a large bowl. Whisk to combine.

With a sharp, thin-bladed knife, carefully slit open one side of each slice of bread to form a pocket, leaving 1 cm (½ inch) around the edges. Spread the mustard on one side of the pocket and place a slice of ham and cheese inside. Put the pockets into a shallow dish. Pour over the egg mixture and leave for 5 minutes, turning once.

Heat a non-stick frying pan over a medium to high heat, add half of the olive oil and swirl to coat the base of the pan. Add two bread pockets, cook on one side for about 2 minutes until golden brown, turn and cook for another minute. Remove from the pan and place on a baking tray. Repeat with the remaining oil and bread pockets. Place the baking tray in the oven and cook for 10 minutes, or until hot and the cheese has melted.

oat, pear and raspberry loaf

MAKES 8 TO 10 SLICES

topping

25 g (1 oz/¼ cup) rolled (porridge) oats

55 g (2 oz/¼ cup) soft brown sugar

2 tablespoons plain (all-purpose) flour

25 g (1 oz) chilled butter, cut into small pieces

cake

100 g (3½ oz/1 cup) rolled (porridge) oats

375 ml (13 fl oz/1½ cups) boiling water

150 g (5½ oz) unsalted butter, diced

115 g (4 oz/½ cup) soft brown sugar

55 g (2 oz/¼ cup) caster (superfine) sugar

2 eggs

1 teaspoon natural vanilla extract

185 g (6½ oz/1½ cups) plain (all-purpose) flour

a pinch of sea salt

1 teaspoon baking powder

2 ripe pears, peeled, cored and diced

60 g (2¼ oz/½ cup) raspberries, fresh or frozen

to serve

butter

Preheat the oven to 180°C (350°F/Gas 4). To make the topping, place all the ingredients into a bowl and rub the butter into the mixture with your fingertips until well incorporated and small clumps form.

To make the cake, place the oats into a bowl and pour over the boiling water. Stir and leave to cool until lukewarm. Cream the butter and sugars in a bowl until pale and creamy. Add the eggs, one at a time, beating well after each addition. Mix in the vanilla. Sift the flour, sea salt and baking powder into the bowl. Drain any excess water off the oats. Add the oats to the mixture and fold to combine. Spread two-thirds of the mixture into a greased or non-stick 19 × 11 cm (7½ × 4¼ inch) loaf (bar) tin. Sprinkle with the pears and raspberries, top with the remaining cake batter then sprinkle the topping over evenly.

Bake for 1 hour 10 minutes, or until a skewer inserted into the centre of the cake comes out clean. Turn out onto a plate before quickly transferring to a wire rack with the topping facing upwards. Leave to cool slightly before cutting. Serve in slices with butter.

mango lassi

125 g (4½ oz/½ cup) plain yoghurt
125 ml (4 fl oz/½ cup) orange juice
1 mango, peeled and cubed
3 large ice cubes

Place all the ingredients in a blender and blend until the mango is well combined. Pour into a tall glass and serve.

raspberry and strawberry smoothie

4 strawberries, hulled
30 g (1 oz/¼ cup) raspberries
15g (½ oz) plain yoghurt
125 ml (4 fl oz/½ cup) milk
3–4 large ice cubes

Place all the ingredients in a blender and blend until smooth. Pour into a tall glass and serve.

real muesli bars

350 g (12 oz/3½ cups) rolled (porridge) oats
30 g (1 oz/½ cup) shredded coconut
50 g (1¾ oz/½ cup) flaked almonds
45 g (1¾ oz/½ cup) wheatgerm
30 g (1 oz/¼ cup) sesame seeds
30 g (1 oz/¼ cup) sunflower seeds
55 g (2 oz/⅓ cup) chopped dried apricots
185 ml (6 fl oz/¾ cup) honey
55 g (2 oz/¼ cup) soft brown sugar
125 ml (4 fl oz/½ cup) vegetable oil

Preheat the oven to 130°C (250°F/Gas 1) and lightly grease and line a 35 x 25 cm (14 x 10 inch) baking tin with baking paper. Put the oats, coconut, almonds, wheatgerm, sesame seeds, sunflower seeds and apricots in a bowl.

Put the honey, sugar and oil in a small saucepan and stir over medium heat until the sugar has dissolved. Pour this over the dry ingredients in the bowl and stir until everything is well combined, mixing with your hands if necessary.

Press the mixture into the tin and bake for 50 minutes, or until golden brown. Cut into bars while still warm.

berry yoghurt muffins

185 g (6½ oz/1½ cups) self-raising flour
150 g (5½ oz/1 cup) wholemeal (whole-wheat) self-raising flour
1 teaspoon ground cinnamon
155 g (5½ oz/¾ cup) soft brown sugar
250 ml (9 fl oz/1 cup) buttermilk
125 g (4½ oz/½ cup) low-fat plain yoghurt
2 eggs, lightly beaten
2 tablespoons vegetable oil
440 g (15½ oz/2 cups) chopped mixed berries (I like strawberries and raspberries)

Preheat the oven to 180°C (350°F/Gas 4). Line a 12-hole 125 ml (4 fl oz/½ cup) capacity muffin tin with paper cases.

Sift the two flours and cinnamon together into a large bowl. Stir in the sugar and then make a well in the centre. Place the buttermilk, yoghurt, eggs and oil into a large bowl and whisk with a fork until just combined. Pour into the well in the dry ingredients and stir with a wooden spoon.

Fold the berries through the mixture (do not overmix or your muffins will be tough). Spoon into the muffin tin and bake for 20 minutes, or until golden.

croque madame

8 slices sourdough bread
butter, to spread on bread, plus
2 teaspoons extra to fry eggs
4 thick slices leg ham
4 slices gruyère or Swiss-style cheese
sea salt
freshly ground black pepper
2 tablespoons olive oil
4 eggs

to serve
shredded fresh flat-leaf (Italian) parsley

Spread four slices of bread with butter and top the unbuttered side with ham, cheese, salt and pepper and another slice of bread to make sandwiches. Butter the top of the sandwich, too.

Heat a large non-stick frying pan over a medium heat. Add half the olive oil and swirl to cover the base of the pan. Put two sandwiches in the pan and put another heavy frying pan on top to squash them down. Cook for 1–2 minutes until they are golden underneath, then flip them over, replace the weight and cook for a couple of minutes more. Use the rest of the oil to cook the other two sandwiches. If you have a panini press, this is the time to use it, as an alternative to frying.

While the sandwiches are cooking, melt half the butter in a separate non-stick frying pan over a medium heat. Crack 2 eggs into the pan, being careful not to break the yolks. Cook the eggs for about 2 minutes, or until just set. Wipe out the frying pan and fry the other 2 eggs in the remaining butter in the same way. Place a fried egg on each sandwich and sprinkle with the parsley.

bacon and egg rolls with spicy tomato relish

SERVES 4

4 large bacon rashers, halved

4 eggs

125 ml (4 fl oz/½ cup) cream

a pinch of salt

20 g (¾ oz) butter

to serve

4 soft bread rolls

rocket (arugula)

spicy tomato relish (see below)

Preheat the oven to 200°C (400°F/Gas 6). Line a large baking tray with baking paper, put the bacon on the tray and bake for 10 minutes, or until crisp. Drain on paper towel.

Meanwhile, whisk together the eggs, cream and salt. Melt the butter in a non-stick frying pan over a high heat, taking care not to let it burn. Pour in the eggs and cook for 20 seconds, or until just set around the edge. With a wooden spoon, gently bring the egg from the outside of the pan to the centre — the idea is to 'fold' rather than scramble the eggs. Leave them to cook for another 20 seconds, then 'fold' again in the same way. When the eggs are just set (remembering that they will continue cooking as they rest) remove from the heat.

Put a couple of pieces of bacon in each roll and top with some egg, rocket leaves and a spoonful of tomato relish.

SPICY TOMATO RELISH

2 tablespoons olive oil

1 onion, finely chopped

2 garlic cloves, thinly sliced

1 red capsicum (pepper), seeded and finely diced

1 green capsicum (pepper), seeded and finely diced

¼ teaspoon cayenne pepper

1 teaspoon paprika

1 fresh red chilli, seeded and finely chopped

2 teaspoons tomato paste (concentrated purée)

a pinch of sugar

1 fresh bay leaf

400 g (14 oz) tin chopped tomatoes

Heat the olive oil in a large saucepan over a medium-low heat. Add the onion and cook, stirring occasionally, for 5 minutes or until soft. Add the garlic and cook, stirring, for another 2–3 minutes.

Add the capsicum and cook, stirring occasionally, for 10 minutes or until soft. Add the spices, chilli and tomato paste and cook, stirring, for 5 minutes. Add the sugar, bay leaf and tomatoes, bring to a low simmer and cook for 40 minutes. Season to taste with salt and pepper before serving.

chocolate-filled french toast

SERVES 4

3 eggs
185 ml (6 fl oz/¾ cup) milk
1 tablespoon caster (superfine) sugar
a pinch of salt
20 g (¾ oz) unsalted butter
8 slices white bread
100 g (3½ oz) milk or dark chocolate, chopped

to serve
icing (confectioners') sugar

Whisk together the eggs, milk, caster sugar and salt in a large, shallow dish. Heat the butter in a large non-stick frying pan over medium heat.

Dip two slices of the bread into the egg mixture, turning them over until they are completely coated. Put them in the frying pan and sprinkle each one with a quarter of the chopped chocolate. Soak another two slices of bread in the egg mixture and put on top of the chocolate bread in the pan to make sandwiches. Press lightly with a spatula to seal the edges.

Cook for 3 minutes each side or until golden brown. Remove from the pan and serve immediately or keep warm while you make the other two sandwiches. Serve dusted with icing sugar.

blueberry breakfast scones

250 g (9 oz/2 cups) plain (all-purpose) flour
1 tablespoon caster (superfine) sugar
3 teaspoons baking powder
a pinch of salt
100 g (3½ oz) cold unsalted butter, cubed
2 eggs, lightly beaten
125 ml (4 fl oz/½ cup) cream
85 g (3 oz/½ cup) blueberries, frozen or fresh, tossed in a little flour
1 egg, whisked with 1 tablespoon milk, for glazing

Preheat the oven to 200°C (400°F/Gas 6) and line a baking tray with baking paper.

Pulse the flour, sugar, baking powder and salt in a food processor until combined. Add the butter and pulse until it is roughly combined (there will still be lumps of butter). Tip into a bowl and mix in the eggs and cream with a knife. Gently mix in the blueberries with your hands (tossing them in a bit of flour first prevents them all sinking to the bottom of the dough).

Turn the dough onto a lightly floured surface and press into a 15 cm (6 inch) square. Cut into quarters and then cut each quarter in half. Place on the baking tray and brush with the egg and milk glaze. Bake for 15–20 minutes or until golden. Serve warm, with butter if you like.

crunchy-top pear muffins

125 g (4½ oz/1 cup) plain
(all-purpose) flour
60 g (2 oz/½ cup) wholemeal
(whole-wheat) flour
3 teaspoons baking powder
2 teaspoons ground cinnamon
100 g (3½ oz/1 cup) rolled oats
140 g (5 oz/¾ cup) brown sugar
2 eggs
250 ml (9 fl oz/1 cup) plain low-fat yoghurt
125 ml (4 fl oz/½ cup) grapeseed oil
(or other light-flavoured oil)
1 pear, peeled and diced
40 g (1½ oz/⅓ cup) pecan nuts,
finely chopped

Preheat the oven to 180°C (350°F/Gas 4) and line six 250 ml (9 fl oz/1 cup) muffin holes with baking paper (or just grease well). Sift the flours, baking powder and cinnamon into a large bowl, add the oats and 100 g (3¼ oz/½ cup) of the brown sugar and stir together. Make a well in the centre.

Whisk together the eggs, yoghurt and oil. Pour into the well in the dry ingredients and stir until just combined. Fold through the pear, being careful not to overmix. Spoon into the muffin tin.

To make the crumble topping, mix the pecans with the remaining brown sugar. Sprinkle over the muffin mixture and then bake for 20–25 minutes until golden brown.

berry hotcakes

165 g (5¾ oz/1¼ cups) frozen mixed berries, thawed

3 tablespoons caster (superfine) sugar

90 g (3¼ oz/¾ cup) plain (all-purpose) flour

90 g (3¼ oz/⅔ cup) wholemeal (whole-wheat) flour

1¼ teaspoons baking powder

a pinch of salt

3 eggs, separated

250 ml (9 fl oz/1 cup) skim milk

125 g (4½ oz/½ cup) fresh ricotta

a little melted butter, for frying

to serve

maple syrup

Lightly mash the berries with a tablespoon of the sugar and set aside.

Sift the flours, baking powder and salt into a large mixing bowl and add the remaining sugar. In a separate bowl, whisk together the egg yolks and milk. Make a well in the centre of the dry ingredients and stir in the egg mixture until just combined. Gently stir in the ricotta.

Beat the egg whites until stiff peaks form. Carefully fold into the batter until just combined. Fold in the berries in two or three strokes to give a marbled effect—do not overmix.

Heat a large frying pan over medium–high heat and brush with a little melted butter. For each hotcake, drop ⅓ cup of the batter into the pan. Cook for 2 minutes, or until bubbles appear on the surface. Turn and cook the other side for 1 minute. Serve with maple syrup.

apple, dried cherry and almond loaf

MAKES 12 SLICES

50 g (1¾ oz/½ cup) rolled (porridge) oats

300 ml (10½ fl oz) milk

250 g (9 oz/2 cups) self-raising flour

1 teaspoon baking powder

125 g (4½ oz) dried cherries

50 g (1¾ oz/ ⅔ cup) dried apple, diced

80 g (2¾ oz/⅓ cup) soft brown sugar

1 teaspoon ground cinnamon

3 tablespoons honey

1 egg, lightly beaten

3 tablespoons roughly chopped raw almonds, plus 2 tablespoons extra

to serve

fresh ricotta cheese

honey

Put the oats in a bowl, pour the milk over them and leave to soak for 30 minutes. Preheat the oven to 180°C (350°F/Gas 4). Lightly grease and line a 1 litre (35 fl oz/4 cups) capacity loaf (bar) tin with baking paper.

Sift the flour and baking powder into a bowl and stir in the rolled oats, dried fruit, sugar, cinnamon, honey, egg and almonds. Mix together well.

Spoon the mixture into the tin, level the top and sprinkle with the extra almonds. Bake the loaf for 45 minutes, or until it is golden brown on top and cooked through. Leave it to cool a little in the tin before turning out onto a wire rack to cool completely. Toast and serve with ricotta cheese and honey.

lunch

Lunch revives the senses. One of the world's best lunches is a fresh baguette with cheese. In winter, however, lunch to me says soup with fresh herbs and a piece of crunchy bread.

I'm not sure if I should admit this, but when I was a little boy I'd sometimes sneak a day off school when I wasn't really sick. Mum was pretty cool about it. We'd go to a local café and have those open sandwiches, which were huge in late seventies Melbourne. Sandwiches you had to eat with a knife and fork seemed like the height of sophistication and were a far cry from the soggy tomato ones I was more familiar with.

If you're entertaining at lunch, you don't need to serve a lot of different things and, although I'm constantly experimenting with new flavours and methods, there's nothing wrong with finding the things you do really well and sticking with them. The most important thing is to be relaxed when entertaining. If you're relaxed, the food will be better.

spicy tomato and fennel soup

2 kg (4lb 8 oz) vine-ripened tomatoes
6 garlic cloves, peeled
I small carrot, diced
½ small fennel bulb, finely chopped
60 ml (2 fl oz/¼ cup) extra virgin olive oil
2 tablespoons sea salt
freshly ground black pepper

to serve
handful of fresh basil leaves (optional)
extra virgin olive oil
ricotta toast (see below)

Preheat the oven to 200°C (400°F/Gas 6). Place the tomatoes, garlic, carrot and fennel in a roasting tin. Drizzle with the olive oil and sprinkle with the salt and pepper. Cover with foil and bake for 1½ hours. Uncover and bake for another 30 minutes, or until the vegetables are well cooked.

Transfer the vegetables to a food processor or blender and blend until combined. What you are looking for is a smoothish mixture with some texture. If you prefer a completely smooth consistency, you can pass the soup through a sieve, but I personally love it with a bit of texture.

Serve in bowls. Top each with basil leaves if you wish and a drizzle of extra virgin olive oil. Serve with ricotta toast.

To make ricotta toast, spread some fresh ricotta cheese on slices of bread, drizzle with olive oil and cook under a hot grill until golden.

60

rice paper roll

2 x 300 g (10½ oz) thick rump steaks
200 g (7 oz) rice vermicelli

marinade
1 fresh lemongrass stalk, white part only,
roughly chopped
3 garlic cloves
1 small fresh red chilli, seeded
60 ml (2 fl oz/¼ cup) fish sauce
1 tablespoon lime juice
2 tablespoons vegetable oil

to serve
1 oak leaf lettuce, washed and dried
bunch of fresh basil
bunch of fresh mint
2 Lebanese (short) cucumbers, halved
lengthways, then thinly sliced on the
diagonal
20 large round rice paper wrappers
Vietnamese dipping sauce (below)

Place all the marinade ingredients with 3 tablespoons water in a food processor or blender and process until smooth. Put the steaks in a bowl and pour the marinade over. Cover with plastic wrap and place in the refrigerator to marinate for 2 hours. Place the rice vermicelli in a bowl and cover with boiling water. Soak for 6–7 minutes, then drain and place on a serving dish.

Place a large frying pan over a high heat until hot. Sear the steaks for 2 minutes on each side, by which time they will be done if you like rare steak. Continue cooking over a medium heat for 1–2 minutes on each side for medium and 2–3 minutes on each side for well done. Remove the steaks and allow to rest for 2 minutes in a warm place. Slice thinly and place on a serving dish.

To serve, arrange the lettuce, basil, mint and cucumber on a large platter and place on the table, alongside the steak, vermicelli, rice paper wrappers and dipping sauce. Place a large bowl of hot water on the table. To wrap the rolls, your guests should first soften the rice paper wrappers in hot water and shake off any excess water. Place the wrapper on a plate, top with a little vermicelli, beef, cucumber, basil and mint in the middle and roll up, tucking in the sides. Place each roll in a lettuce leaf and dip into sauce.

VIETNAMESE DIPPING SAUCE
Place all the ingredients in a bowl and stir until the sugar is dissolved.

60 ml (2 fl oz/¼ cup) fish sauce
60 ml (2 fl oz/¼ cup) lime juice
2 tablespoons rice vinegar
1 tablespoon caster (superfine) sugar
1 garlic clove, finely chopped
1 large fresh red chilli, seeded and finely
chopped

If you don't have rice vinegar, just use extra lime juice to taste. You're looking for a balance of sweet, salty and sour.

crab and asparagus risotto

SERVES 4

1.5 litres (52 fl oz/6 cups) chicken or fish stock
1 tablespoon extra virgin olive oil
1 small onion, finely diced
1 teaspoon sea salt
50 g (1¾ oz) butter
330 g (11¾ oz/1½ cups) arborio rice
8 asparagus spears, finely sliced on the diagonal
250 g (9 oz) cooked fresh crabmeat
grated zest of 1 lemon
60 ml (2 fl oz/¼ cup) lemon juice
sea salt, extra, to taste
freshly ground black pepper
fresh chervil sprigs, for garnishing

Pour the stock into a saucepan and bring to the boil. Reduce the heat and keep at simmering point.

Place a large heavy-based saucepan over a medium heat and add the oil, onion, salt and half the butter. Stir until the onion is translucent. Add the rice and stir for 1–2 minutes, until the rice is well coated. Add a cupful of stock at a time, stirring constantly and being sure that each addition of stock is absorbed before you add more.

Continue adding the stock for about 25 minutes. Add the asparagus and continue to add the remaining stock for about another 2 minutes, or until the rice is *al dente* and creamy. Remove the saucepan from the heat, stir in the remaining butter, the crabmeat, lemon zest and juice, and salt and pepper, to taste. Cover the saucepan and leave to sit for 3 minutes to allow the flavours to develop. Stir and divide among four bowls. Top with the chervil sprigs.

Although I've used arborio rice here, you can use other risotto rices such as vialone nano or carnaroli.

zucchini fritters with yoghurt sauce

500 g (1 lb 2 oz) zucchini (courgettes), grated
½ teaspoon sea salt
8 spring onions (scallions), chopped
125 g (4½ oz) feta cheese, crumbled
15 g (½ oz/ ½ cup) fresh flat-leaf (Italian) parsley, chopped
15 g (¼ cup) fresh mint, chopped
2 eggs, lightly beaten
60 g (2¼ oz/½ cup) plain (all-purpose) flour
sea salt, extra, to taste
freshly ground black pepper
60 ml (2 fl oz/¼ cup) olive oil, for shallow-frying

to serve
yoghurt sauce (see below)
lime wedges

Put the zucchini in a colander, sprinkle with the sea salt, toss lightly and set aside for 30 minutes. Squeeze out the excess liquid from the zucchini and pat dry with paper towels.

Put the zucchini, spring onion, feta, parsley, mint and eggs in a bowl and stir lightly to combine. Stir in the flour, and season with salt and pepper.

Heat the oil in a non-stick frying pan over a medium to high heat. Drop tablespoons of the batter into the hot oil, flattening gently with the back of a spoon. Cook for 2 minutes on each side, or until golden brown. Drain on paper towels and serve with the yoghurt sauce and lime wedges.

YOGHURT SAUCE

Put all the ingredients in a bowl and stir to combine.

1 garlic clove, finely minced
1 tablespoon extra virgin olive oil
125 g (4½ oz/½ cup) plain yoghurt
2 tablespoons lemon juice
sea salt
freshly ground black pepper

prawn and rice vermicelli salad

250 g (9 oz) rice vermicelli
125 ml (4 fl oz/½ cup) soy sauce
60 ml (2 fl oz/¼ cup) rice vinegar
3 teaspoons oil mixed with 1 finely sliced
large fresh red chilli
1½ tablespoons sugar
1½ tablespoons peanut oil
3 x 4 cm (1¼ x 1½ inch) piece of fresh
ginger, finely julienned
12 cooked prawns (shrimp), peeled,
deveined, and sliced in half lengthways
2 Lebanese short cucumbers, julienned
4 spring onions (scallions), finely sliced
on the diagonal

to serve
¼ cup fresh coriander (cilantro) sprigs
¼ cup fresh mint sprigs
lime wedges

Put the rice vermicelli in a bowl and pour in enough boiling water to cover. Soak for 6–7 minutes, then drain and refresh under cold water before draining thoroughly.

Stir the soy sauce, rice vinegar, chilli oil, sugar, peanut oil and ginger together in a large bowl until the sugar is dissolved. Add the noodles, prawns, cucumber and spring onion and stir carefully to combine.

Divide among four plates and top with coriander and mint. Serve with lime wedges.

crispy-skinned salmon with fresh noodle salad and soy dressing

SERVES 4

400 g (14 oz) fresh coriander (cilantro) egg
noodles or other fresh egg noodles
4 salmon fillets, 2.5 cm (1 inch) thick,
skin on
2 tablespoons oil
sea salt
freshly ground black pepper
1 cucumber, finely julienned
110 g (3¾ oz/1 cup) finely julienned daikon
radish
2 spring onions (scallions), finely sliced
on the diagonal
soy dressing (see below)

to serve
lime wedges

2 teaspoons sesame oil
125 ml (4 fl oz/½ cup) soy sauce
1½ tablespoons balsamic vinegar
2 tablespoons caster (superfine) sugar
60 ml (2 fl oz/¼ cup) lime juice
2 small fresh red chillies, finely chopped
(optional)

Bring a large saucepan of water to the boil over a high heat, add the noodles and blanch for 1 minute. Refresh under cold water.

Heat a frying pan over a high heat for 2 minutes. Brush the salmon fillets with the oil and season liberally with the salt and pepper. Cook the salmon with the skin side down for 2 minutes, then turn over and cook for another 2 minutes. Remove from the pan and allow to rest for 2 minutes. The salmon should be quite rare and the skin crispy.

To assemble the salad, divide the noodles among four plates. Arrange the cucumber and daikon over the noodles and sprinkle with spring onion. Put a salmon fillet on each plate and drizzle with soy dressing. Serve with lime wedges.

SOY DRESSING
Stir all the dressing ingredients together in a bowl until the sugar is dissolved.

spiced zucchini soup

SERVES 4

2 small white onions, or 1 large white
onion, roughly chopped
1 tablespoon olive oil
a pinch of sea salt
1 tablespoon curry powder
1 kg (2 lb 4 oz) zucchini (courgettes),
sliced
1.5 litres (52 fl oz/6 cups) vegetable or
chicken stock
freshly ground black pepper
55 g (2 oz/¼ cup) short-grain rice

to serve
plain yoghurt
1 zucchini (courgette), shaved into thin
ribbons and lightly blanched

Place the onion, olive oil and salt in a large saucepan over a medium to high heat and cook for 5 minutes, or until the onion is translucent. Add the curry powder and cook for 2 minutes. Add the zucchini, stock, pepper and rice and bring to the boil. Reduce the heat to low and cook for another 20 minutes.

Blend the soup in a blender or food processor until smooth. Serve immediately with a dollop of yoghurt and garnish with zucchini ribbons.

prawn skewers with rice salad

3 thick slices sourdough or wholemeal bread, crusts removed

80 ml (2½ fl oz/⅓ cup) extra virgin olive oil

24 medium raw prawns (shrimp), peeled and deveined

2 garlic cloves, crushed

¼ cup fresh flat-leaf (Italian) parsley, finely chopped

finely grated zest of 1 lemon

1 teaspoon sea salt

freshly ground black pepper

to serve

lemon wedges

rice salad (see below)

Soak eight wooden skewers in water for 30 minutes to stop them from burning during cooking. Preheat the oven to 200°C (400°F/ Gas 6). Place the bread on a baking tray and toast for 20 minutes, or until lightly golden. Remove from the oven and leave to cool. Crumble the toasted bread with your hands or process in a food processor until breadcrumbs form.

Place the olive oil and prawns in a large bowl and toss to combine. Add the remaining ingredients and stir thoroughly so that each prawn is evenly coated with breadcrumbs. Cover with plastic wrap and refrigerate for 30 minutes. Preheat a grill (broiler) to high. Thread 3 prawns on each skewer, curling and skewering the tails to maintain a round shape.

Place on a baking tray and cook for 2 minutes each side, or until golden. Serve with lemon wedges and the rice salad.

RICE SALAD

60 ml (2 fl oz/¼ cup) olive oil

2 tablespoons lemon juice

a pinch of sea salt

freshly ground black pepper

740 g (1lb 10 oz/4 cups) cooked short-grain rice

1 tablespoon lemon zest

½ red onion, finely diced

⅓ cup fresh flat-leaf (Italian) parsley, roughly chopped

2 celery stalks, finely diced

75 g (⅓ cup) green olives, pitted and sliced

Combine the oil, lemon juice, salt and pepper in a serving bowl. Add the remaining ingredients and toss until well combined.

This rice salad can be made ahead of time and refrigerated. If cooking the rice ahead of time, cool down quickly and refrigerate until required. Stand at room temperature for 15 minutes before serving.

vietnamese chicken salad

3 x 200 g (7 oz) chicken breasts, skin on

2 tablespoons vegetable oil

a pinch of sea salt

pepper (I like white pepper in this salad, but use black if that is all you have)

90 g (3¼ oz/1 cup) bean sprouts

1 cup fresh Vietnamese mint leaves

1 cup fresh Asian basil leaves, or fresh basil leaves

180 g (6¼ oz/4 cups) Chinese cabbage, finely shredded

Vietnamese dressing (see below)

90 g (3¼ oz/1 cup) pickled carrot (see below), or raw carrot, peeled and finely julienned

60 ml (2 fl oz/¼ cup) lime juice

60 ml (2 fl oz/¼ cup) fish sauce

2 tablespoons rice vinegar

1 tablespoon caster (superfine) sugar

2 garlic cloves, very finely chopped

3 red Asian shallots, or ½ red onion, finely sliced

2 small fresh red chillies, very finely chopped (seeds removed, if you don't like the heat)

250 g (9 oz) carrots, peeled and finely julienned

1 teaspoon sea salt

2 tablespoons rice vinegar

1 tablespoon caster (superfine) sugar

Preheat the oven to 220°C (425°F/Gas 7). Heat a frying pan over a high heat, and while the pan is heating, brush the chicken with the oil and season with salt and pepper.

Place the chicken skin-side down and sear for 2 minutes, turn and sear for another minute. Put the chicken on a baking tray and cook in the oven for 8–10 minutes. Leave to rest for 20 minutes. Shred the chicken into thin strips with your hands and place in a large bowl. Add the remaining ingredients and toss to combine.

VIETNAMESE DRESSING

Place all the ingredients in a small bowl and stir until the sugar is dissolved.

PICKLED CARROT

Place the carrots in a colander, sprinkle with the salt and toss to combine. Leave for 20 minutes. While the carrot is resting, place 185 ml (6 fl oz/¾ cup) water with the vinegar and sugar in a small saucepan over a medium heat and bring to the boil. Remove from the heat and cool. Rinse the carrot, squeezing out any excess water, and place in a bowl. Pour over the pickling liquid and stand for 1 hour. Strain before serving.

burger with hummus and potato wedges

4 good-quality hamburger buns or rolls

500 g (1 lb 2 oz) lean minced (ground) beef

1 red onion, grated

a pinch of sea salt

freshly ground black pepper

3 tablespoons olive oil

250 g (9 oz) cherry tomatoes, sliced

½ teaspoon sumac

1 small white salad onion, cut into thin wedges

¼ cup fresh (flat-leaf) Italian parsley, shredded

1 tablespoon lemon juice

hummus (see below)

potato wedges (see below)

Cut the buns horizontally into halves. Put the mince, onion, salt and pepper in a bowl and combine well with your hands. Form into four patties, making them slightly larger than the buns because they will shrink during cooking.

Heat 2 tablespoons of the oil in a large non-stick frying pan over a medium to high heat, add the hamburger patties and, because the patties tend to puff up, make a small dip in the centre of each with the back of a spoon. Cook for 4 minutes on each side, or until done to your liking.

Make the salad by tossing the cherry tomatoes, sumac, onion and parsley together with the remaining olive oil and the lemon juice. While the burgers are cooking, toast the buns with the cut side up. Spread hummus on the toasted sides, then top with a patty, salad and the bun tops. Serve with potato wedges.

HUMMUS

400 g (14 oz) tin chickpeas, drained

1 garlic clove

2 tablespoons lemon juice

sea salt

freshly ground black pepper

Process the chickpeas, garlic and lemon juice in a food processor with 3 tablespoons of water until the hummus is smooth. Season, to taste, with salt and pepper.

POTATO WEDGES

1½ tablespoons vegetable oil

5 garlic cloves, unpeeled and crushed

1½ tablespoons lime juice

2 teaspoons Tabasco sauce

500 g (1 lb) potatoes, unpeeled, scrubbed, dried and cut into wedges

freshly ground black pepper

sea salt

Preheat the oven to 200°C (400°F/Gas 6). Put the oil, garlic, lime juice and Tabasco sauce in a large bowl and whisk to combine. Add the potatoes and pepper and stir until the potatoes are coated. Transfer to a baking dish, spreading the potatoes evenly over the dish with the rounded side down. Bake for 45 minutes, or until crispy. Sprinkle with sea salt and serve.

warm tomato and ricotta pasta salad

500 g (1 lb 2 oz) cherry tomatoes, cut in half
125 ml (4 fl oz/½ cup) extra virgin olive oil
60 ml (2 fl oz/¼ cup) red wine vinegar
½ teaspoon caster (superfine) sugar
1 teaspoon sea salt
freshly ground black pepper
4 thick slices wholemeal (whole wheat) or sourdough bread
1 garlic clove, sliced in half
500 g (1 lb 2 oz) rigatoni
1 cup fresh basil leaves, finely shredded
250 g (9 oz/1 cup) fresh ricotta cheese

Preheat the oven to 200°C (400°F/Gas 6). Place the tomatoes, 80 ml (2½ fl oz/⅓ cup) of the olive oil, the vinegar and sugar in a large bowl and stir to combine. Season with the salt and pepper. Cover and leave to marinate while you prepare the rest of the dish.

Rub the bread on both sides with the cut side of the garlic. Brush with the remaining olive oil and sprinkle with salt. Put the bread on a baking tray and place in the oven. Cook for 20 minutes, or until crisp. Remove from the oven and crumble into coarse breadcrumbs with your hands. Set aside.

Cook the pasta in a large saucepan of rapidly boiling salted water until *al dente*. Drain well, then add to the tomatoes. Add the basil and toss to combine.

Divide the pasta between four serving plates, or put it on one large serving dish, crumble over the ricotta cheese and sprinkle with the breadcrumbs.

chorizo, potato and red capsicum frittata

SERVES 4

1½ tablespoons olive oil
1 chorizo sausage, sliced
1 red-skinned potato, diced
1 small onion, diced
1 red capsicum (pepper), diced
10 eggs
2 tablespoons fresh flat-leaf
(Italian) parsley, chopped
2 tablespoons finely grated
parmesan cheese

Heat 2 teaspoons of the olive oil in a 20 cm (8 inch) frying pan over medium-high heat and cook the chorizo, stirring occasionally, for 5–6 minutes, or until crisp. Drain on paper towel.

Turn the heat to medium, add the remaining oil, the potato and onion to the pan and cook, stirring occasionally, for 5 minutes, or until the onion is soft. Add the capsicum and cook for 5 minutes before returning the chorizo to the pan. Preheat your grill (broiler) to hot.

Whisk the eggs and pour into the pan. Reduce the heat to low, cover the pan and cook until the eggs have almost set. Sprinkle with parsley and parmesan cheese and then put the pan under the grill for 3–4 minutes until the frittata is golden and puffed.

spaghettini with lemon, prosciutto and chilli

SERVES 4

60 ml (2 fl oz/¼ cup) lemon juice
60 ml (2 fl oz/¼ cup) extra virgin olive oil
2 small fresh red chillies, seeded and
finely chopped
a pinch of sea salt
freshly ground black pepper
12 slices prosciutto, cut into thin strips
1 tablespoon grated lemon zest
250 g (9 oz) rocket (arugula)
leaves, shredded
400 g (14 oz) good-quality dried
thin spaghettini

Whisk the lemon juice, olive oil, chilli, salt and pepper in a bowl to blend.

Put the prosciutto, lemon zest and the rocket in a bowl and toss to combine.

Bring a large saucepan of salted water to the boil. Add the spaghettini and cook until *al dente*. Drain and add to the prosciutto and rocket. Pour the dressing over and toss to combine.

Transfer to a large serving dish or divide among four bowls.

Remember, with simple recipes such as this one, you can throw in any of your favourite ingredients.

citrus risotto with garlic chilli prawns

SERVES 4

1.5 litres (52 fl oz/6 cups) chicken stock
1 tablespoon olive oil
1 small onion, finely diced
1 teaspoon sea salt
50 g (1¾ oz) butter
330 g (11¾ oz/1½ cups) arborio rice
finely grated zest of 1 lemon
1 tablespoon lemon juice
freshly ground black pepper
2 small fresh red chillies
2 garlic cloves
2 tablespoons olive oil, extra
20 raw prawns (shrimp), peeled and
deveined, with tails intact

to serve
¼ cup flat-leaf (Italian) parsley, roughly
chopped
lemon wedges

Place the stock in a large saucepan and bring to the boil over a high heat. Reduce the heat and keep at simmering point. Place a large heavy-based saucepan over a medium heat and add the olive oil, onion, salt and half of the butter. Stir until the onion is translucent. Add the rice and stir for 1–2 minutes, or until the rice is well coated.

Gradually add the simmering stock, a cupful at a time, stirring constantly and making sure the stock is absorbed before you add more. This should take 20 minutes and the rice should be *al dente*. and creamy. Remove the saucepan from the heat, then stir in the remaining butter, lemon zest, lemon juice and pepper to taste. Cover the saucepan and leave to sit for 3 minutes for the flavours to develop.

Meanwhile, pound the chilli and garlic in a mortar and pestle. Place the extra olive oil in a frying pan over a high heat and heat until hot. Season the prawns with salt and pepper. Cook for 2 minutes, shaking the pan, until the prawns are just opaque then add the chilli and garlic and cook for 1 minute. Remove from the heat and set aside.

Stir the risotto and divide between four bowls. Toss the prawns with the parsley then place on top of the risotto. Serve with lemon wedges.

briget's onion and feta cheese tart

SERVES 6

2 tablespoons olive oil

1 kg (2 lb 4 oz) onions, finely sliced

1 tablespoon soft brown sugar

2 tablespoons balsamic vinegar

1 teaspoon sea salt

freshly ground black pepper

1 x 375 g (13 oz) block puff pastry

50 g (1¾ oz/½ cup) finely grated parmesan cheese

150 g (5½ oz/1 cup) feta cheese, crumbled

2 tablespoons oregano leaves

Place the olive oil and onion in a saucepan over a medium heat and cook for 20 minutes, stirring occasionally. Add the sugar, balsamic vinegar, salt and pepper. Cook for another 5 minutes, or until the onion is soft and caramelised. Remove from the heat and set aside to cool.

Meanwhile, preheat the oven to 220°C (425°F/Gas 7). Roll out the pastry to a 20 x 40 cm (8 x 16 inch) rectangle on a lightly floured surface. Trim the edges with a sharp knife and place on a baking tray lined with baking paper. Score a 1 cm (½ inch) border around the edge of the pastry, taking care not to cut all the way through to the bottom. Prick the pastry with a fork and sprinkle the parmesan cheese within the scored edges.

Place the onion on top of the parmesan. Bake in the oven for 20–25 minutes, or until the pastry is puffed and golden brown. Remove from the oven and sprinkle with the feta cheese and oregano leaves.

tagliatelle with chicken and green beans

SERVES 4

2 x 200 g (7 oz) chicken breasts, thinly sliced
2 tablespoons extra virgin olive oil
3 garlic cloves, fsliced
sea salt
freshly ground black pepper
375 g (13 oz) tagliatelle (I like to use fresh spinach tagliatelle, but plain fresh pasta will be just as delicious)
2 tablespoons olive oil
200 g (7 oz) baby green beans, topped (not tailed) and sliced from end to end, on the diagonal
125 ml (4 fl oz/½ cup) chicken stock
good-quality parmesan cheese, grated
¼ cup fresh basil leaves

Place the chicken, extra virgin olive oil and garlic in a bowl and stir to combine. Season with the salt and pepper. Cook the pasta in a large saucepan of rapidly boiling salted water until *al dente* and drain well.

Meanwhile, when the pasta is almost ready, place a large frying pan over a high heat until hot. Add the extra olive oil and heat for 5 seconds. Add the chicken with the marinade and sear quickly for 30 seconds. Add the beans and reduce the heat to medium. Cook for another 2 minutes, stirring occasionally. Return the heat to high, add the stock and simmer for 30 seconds. Add the pasta and toss to combine.

Divide the pasta evenly between four bowls and top with the freshly grated parmesan cheese and basil.

barbecued duck salad

1 Chinese roast duck

6 spring onions (scallions), sliced on the diagonal

2 Lebanese (short) cucumbers, julienned

1 cup fresh coriander (cilantro) leaves

1 large fresh red chilli, thinly sliced

to serve

dressing (see below)

steamed rice

2½ tablespoons hoisin sauce

2 tablespoons soy sauce

1 tablespoon balsamic vinegar

2 teaspoons sesame oil

Pull the skin and meat from the duck with your fingers, roughly shredding both. Place the duck, spring onion, cucumber, coriander and chilli in a bowl and toss to combine. Drizzle over the dressing just before serving with steamed rice, or serve alongside.

DRESSING

Place all the ingredients in a bowl and stir to combine.

I buy my roast ducks in Chinatown at a Chinese barbecue shop.

pan-fried fish with lemon potato salad

SERVES 4

olive oil, for greasing the pan

4 x 200 g (7 oz) firm white fish fillets, such as snapper, skin removed

to serve

lemon wedges

mint leaves

lemon potato salad (see below)

750 g (1 lb 10 oz) waxy potatoes, such as kipfler, peeled and sliced

1 teaspoon sea salt

80 ml (2½ fl oz/⅓ cup) extra virgin olive oil

125 ml (4 fl oz/½ cup) lemon juice

1 teaspoon sumac (optional)

freshly ground black pepper

1 small green capsicum (pepper), finely diced

2 large fresh red chillies, seeded and finely diced

¼ cup fresh mint, chopped

1½ cups fresh flat-leaf (Italian) parsley, thinly sliced

6 spring onions (scallions), thinly sliced

Heat a little oil in a large non-stick frying pan over a medium to high heat until hot. Add the fish and cook for 3 minutes. Turn and cook on the other side for 2–3 minutes, or until the fish is opaque and just cooked. Garnish with mint leaves and serve with lemon wedges and the lemon potato salad.

LEMON POTATO SALAD

Bring a large saucepan of water to the boil over a high heat. Add the potatoes and salt, reduce the heat to medium and simmer for about 8–10 minutes until the potatoes are tender when pierced with a knife. Remember to undercook the potatoes a little, because they will continue cooking when removed from the water.

Place the olive oil, lemon juice and sumac in a bowl and stir to combine. Season with salt and pepper. Pour half the dressing over the hot potatoes and stir gently. Leave to cool.

Add the capsicum, chilli, mint, parsley, spring onion and remaining dressing and stir gently.

A nice alternative is to make a simple herb crust by mixing chopped parsley and coriander with chilli, lemon zest, salt, pepper and olive oil. Press firmly on the fish, refrigerate for 30 minutes then cook as above.

97

spaghetti with cherry tomatoes, ricotta, spinach and pecorino

SERVES 4

750 g (1 lb 10 oz/5 cups) cherry tomatoes

4 garlic cloves, sliced

1 red onion, thinly sliced

small handful of fresh oregano

100 ml (3½ fl oz) extra virgin olive oil

500 g (1 lb 2 oz) fresh spaghetti

50 g (1¾ oz) baby English spinach leaves

200 g (7 oz) fresh ricotta cheese

freshly ground black pepper

to serve

75 g (2½ oz) pecorino cheese, grated

Preheat the oven to 180°C (350°F/Gas 4). Put the tomatoes, garlic, onion and oregano on a baking tray and drizzle with the oil. Roast for 20–25 minutes or until wilted.

Cook the pasta in a large saucepan of boiling salted water until *al dente*. Drain and toss with the tomato mixture, spinach and half of the ricotta. Divide among serving bowls and top with the remaining ricotta cheese and some freshly ground pepper. Serve with the grated pecorino cheese.

I really like to use pecorino sometimes, rather than the more obvious parmesan. Pecorino is an Italian sheep's milk cheese.

penne with eggplant and chilli

SERVES 4

1 large eggplant (aubergine), sliced
80 ml (2½ fl oz/⅓ cup) olive oil
sea salt
4 garlic cloves, thinly sliced
2 large fresh red chillies, thinly sliced
2 x 400 g (14 oz) tins chopped tomatoes
freshly ground black pepper
500 g (1 lb 2 oz) penne
small handful of fresh flat-leaf (Italian)
parsley, chopped

Preheat the grill (broiler). Arrange the eggplant on a baking tray, brush liberally with half of the oil and sprinkle with salt on both sides. Grill for 3–6 minutes on each side or until golden brown and cooked. When the eggplant is cool enough to handle, cut into small cubes.

Meanwhile, place a frying pan over medium heat. Add the rest of the oil and sauté the garlic, chilli and a little salt for 1 minute. Add the tomatoes and pepper and simmer for 10–15 minutes. Gently fold through the eggplant.

Meanwhile, cook the pasta in a large saucepan of boiling salted water until *al dente*. Drain well and toss with the sauce and parsley.

spicy pumpkin soup

SERVES 4

1 tablespoon olive oil

1 red onion, sliced

2.5 cm (1 inch) piece of fresh ginger, sliced

2 teaspoons Thai red curry paste

1.6 kg (3 lb 8 oz) butternut pumpkin (squash), peeled, seeded and cubed

170 ml (5½ fl oz/⅔ cup) coconut milk

1 tablespoon fish sauce

1 tablespoon lime juice

1–2 teaspoons sugar, or to taste

to serve

small handful of fresh oriander (cilantro) leaves, shredded

Place a large saucepan over medium heat. Add the olive oil, onion, ginger and curry paste and cook for 1 minute until fragrant. Add the pumpkin and stir to coat with the paste. Add 1 litre (35 fl oz/4 cups) of water and bring to the boil. Reduce the heat and simmer for 30 minutes or until the pumpkin is tender.

Transfer to a blender and mix until smooth. Return to the pan, stir in the coconut milk and season with the fish sauce, lime juice and sugar. Heat through gently before serving. Top with the coriander leaves.

Soup is always good to make in bulk because it's so easy to freeze — just don't add the coriander until after you've reheated or it will discolour.

haloumi
open sandwich

MAKES 4

1 tablespoon olive oil
8 x 1 cm (½ inch) thick slices haloumi
cheese
½ lemon
4 slices sourdough bread
4 tablespoons hummus
1 Lebanese (short) cucumber, cut into
long wedges
rocket (arugula) leaves
1 red capsicum (pepper), roasted, peeled
and cut into quarters
freshly ground black pepper

Heat the olive oil in a large non-stick frying pan over high heat. Add the haloumi and cook for 2 minutes on each side, or until golden brown. Remove from the pan and squeeze with a little lemon juice.

Toast the sourdough and spread with hummus. Top each slice with some cucumber, rocket leaves, roasted capsicum and haloumi. Season generously with black pepper.

chickpea stew with tomatoes and green chilli

SERVES 4 AS A MAIN OR 8 AS A SIDE

2 tablespoons olive oil

1 red onion, thinly sliced

3 garlic cloves, thinly sliced

2 teaspoons fresh ginger, grated

1 or 2 fresh green chillies, to taste, seeded and finely chopped

1 teaspoon sea salt

2 x 400 g (14 oz) tins chickpeas, rinsed

1 teaspoon ground cumin

½ teaspoon turmeric (optional)

freshly ground black pepper

500 g (1 lb 2 oz) cherry tomatoes, halved

100 g (3½ oz/2¼ cups) baby English spinach leaves

to serve

plain yoghurt

Heat a large deep frying pan over a medium to high heat. Add the oil, onion, garlic, ginger, chilli and salt. Cook, stirring, for 5 minutes, or until the onions are soft. Add the chickpeas, 80 ml (2½ fl oz/⅓ cup) water, cumin, turmeric, if using, and pepper and cook for 5 minutes, or until the water evaporates. Add the tomatoes and cook for another 2 minutes to soften. Remove from the heat and taste for seasoning. Stir through the spinach and top with yoghurt.

I like to serve this dish with pitta crisps — just break up pieces of pitta bread, drizzle with olive oil, sea salt, black pepper and paprika and bake for 10–12 minutes in a moderate oven until crisp.

107

L.A. burger with sweet potato fries

SERVES 4

500 g (1 lb 2 oz) minced (ground) pork

½ onion, grated

½ teaspoon fennel seeds, lightly toasted and crushed

40 g (1½ oz/½ cup) fresh white breadcrumbs

1 egg, lightly beaten

1 tablespoon fresh flat-leaf (Italian) parsley, chopped

sea salt

freshly ground black pepper

to serve

hamburger buns

rocket (arugula) leaves

roasted red capsicum (pepper)

1 red onion, thinly sliced

sweet potato fries (see below)

1 kg (2 lb 4 oz) sweet potatoes, peeled and cut into batons

2 tablespoons olive oil

2 teaspoons paprika

¼ teaspoon cayenne pepper

sea salt

Put the pork, onion, fennel, breadcrumbs, egg and parsley in a large mixing bowl. Season well with salt and pepper and then use your hands to mix everything together thoroughly. Shape the mixture into four patties, then cover and leave in the fridge for 30 minutes.

Heat a frying pan or chargrill pan over high heat. Add the patties and cook for 4–5 minutes on each side until they are browned and cooked through.

Place the patties in hamburger buns and top with rocket leaves, roasted capsicum and a few slices of red onion. Serve with sweet potato fries.

SWEET POTATO FRIES

Preheat the oven to 230°C (450°F/Gas 8). Toss the sweet potato batons with the olive oil, paprika, cayenne pepper and sea salt. Scatter them in a single layer on a large baking tray and bake for 30 minutes, turning occasionally, until the fries are golden brown.

SERVES 4 # salmon tartine

90 g (3¼ oz/½ cup) whole green olives,
flesh sliced from the pit
1 lemon, peel and pith removed, cut into
segments
1 tablespoon small salted capers, rinsed
large handful of fresh flat-leaf (Italian)
parsley
8 slices sourdough bread
160 g (5¾ oz/⅔ cup) fresh ricotta cheese
200 g (7 oz) smoked salmon

Gently toss together the olives, lemon segments, capers and parsley. Toast the sourdough bread until golden. Spread the bread with ricotta and top with smoked salmon. Arrange two slices on each plate and top with some of the olive mixture. Serve immediately.

vegetable soup

30 g (1 oz) butter

1 large leek, white part only, thinly sliced

2 celery stalks, diced

2 large red-skinned potatoes, diced

1 turnip, peeled and diced

1.5 litres (52 fl oz/6 cups) vegetable stock

sea salt

freshly ground black pepper

80 g (3 oz/½ cup) small pasta
(such as macaroni)

1 large zucchini (courgette), diced

150 g (5½ oz/1 cup) green beans, topped
and cut into short lengths

155 g (5½ oz/1 cup) fresh peas

Melt the butter in a large saucepan over medium heat. Add the leek, celery, potato and turnip and cook, stirring frequently, for 5 minutes. Add the vegetable stock, salt and pepper and bring to the boil. Lower the heat and add the remaining ingredients. Simmer gently for 8 minutes until the pasta is cooked and the vegetables are just tender. Ladle into bowls and top with lots of freshly ground black pepper.

roast beef sandwiches with olive caper relish

SERVES 8 WITH LEFTOVERS

1.5 kg (3 lb 5 oz) piece of beef topside
olive oil, to drizzle
sea salt
freshly ground black pepper

to serve
sourdough bread, or your favourite sandwich bread
rocket (arugula) leaves
olive caper relish (see below)

Preheat the oven to 220°C (425°F/Gas 7). Put the beef on a large baking tray, drizzle with olive oil and season with the salt and pepper. Roast for 15 minutes, or until browned.

Reduce the oven temperature to 200°C (400°F/Gas 6) and roast the beef for a further 45 minutes (it will be medium-rare). Remove from the oven, cover loosely with foil and set aside to rest for 30 minutes. Thinly slice the beef and use to make sandwiches with the bread, rocket and olive caper relish.

125 g (4½ oz/cup) pitted green olives
1 tablespoon small salted capers, rinsed
2 tablespoons fresh flat-leaf (Italian) parsley, chopped
2 teaspoons grated lemon zest
3 tablespoons extra virgin olive oil
freshly ground black pepper

OLIVE CAPER RELISH

Put the olives, capers, parsley and lemon zest in a food processor and process until finely chopped. Add the olive oil and process until the relish has a coarse pesto-like consistency. Season with the pepper.

poached salmon and risoni salad

1 tablespoon sea salt
½ teaspoon white peppercorns
1 fresh bay leaf
400 g (14 oz) salmon fillets, skin removed
200 g (7 oz) risoni
80 g (2¾ oz/½ cup) peas (frozen are fine)
grated zest and juice of 1 lemon
55 g (2 oz/1¼ cups) baby spinach leaves
2 tablespoons fresh flat-leaf (Italian) parsley, chopped
2 teaspoons fresh dill, chopped
1 tablespoon extra virgin olive oil
a large pinch of caster (superfine) sugar
sea salt
freshly ground black pepper

Put the salt, peppercorns and bay leaf in a large, deep frying pan with 750 ml (26 fl oz/3 cups) of water and bring to the boil. Simmer for 5 minutes, then remove from the heat. Add the salmon, cover and leave for 15 minutes. Lift the fish carefully out of the stock. When cool enough to handle, flake the fish into pieces, picking out any bones.

Cook the risoni in a large saucepan of boiling salted water until *al dente*, adding the peas and lemon zest for the last 2 minutes of cooking. Rinse under cold running water and drain well.

Put the risoni , salmon, spinach, parsley and dill in a large bowl. Whisk together the lemon juice, olive oil and sugar to make a dressing. Add the dressing to the salad and toss gently. Season with salt and pepper.

spaghetti with asparagus, mint and chilli

SERVES 4

400 g (14 oz) spaghetti
80 ml (2¾ fl oz/⅓ cup) extra virgin olive oil
3 garlic cloves, thinly sliced
1 large fresh red chilli, seeded and thinly sliced
2 bunches of asparagus (about 400 g/14 oz), thinly sliced
handful of fresh mint leaves
sea salt
freshly ground black pepper

to serve
grated parmesan cheese

Cook the spaghetti in a large saucepan of boiling salted water until *al dente*. Reserve half a cupful of the cooking liquid before draining the pasta.

Meanwhile, heat the olive oil in a large, deep frying pan over medium heat. Add the garlic and chilli and cook, stirring, for 30 seconds. Add the asparagus and continue to cook, stirring, for 1–2 minutes or until it is bright green and just tender. Add the pasta cooking liquid and simmer for 30 seconds.

Add the hot pasta and mint leaves to the asparagus and toss together. Season and serve immediately with the grated parmesan cheese.

pork, veal and pistachio sausage rolls

1 tablespoon olive oil
1 large onion, finely chopped
2 garlic cloves, crushed
2 teaspoons ground cumin
1 teaspoon ground coriander
500 g (1 lb 2 oz) minced (ground) veal
500 g (1 lb 2 oz) minced (ground) pork
70 g (2½ oz/½ cup) roughly chopped pistachio nuts
1 egg
sea salt
freshly ground black pepper
4 sheets puff pastry
2 egg yolks
2 tablespoons milk
sesame seeds, to sprinkle

Preheat the oven to 200°C (400°F/Gas 6) and line a large baking tray with baking paper.

Heat the olive oil in a frying pan over a medium heat. Add the onion and cook, stirring occasionally, for 5–6 minutes until softened. Add the garlic and spices and cook, stirring, for another minute.

Set aside to cool, then tip into a large bowl. Add the veal, pork, pistachios and egg and mix with your hands until thoroughly combined. Season with sea salt and freshly ground black pepper.

Cut each pastry sheet in half, so you have eight pieces. Working with one piece of pastry at a time, spread an eighth of the filling down the middle of the pastry in a log shape.

Mix together the egg yolks and milk and brush around the outside edges of each piece of pastry. Roll up and cut each roll into two pieces. Place on the baking tray with the sealed edges underneath.

Brush the tops of the sausage rolls with the egg wash and sprinkle with sesame seeds. Bake for 25–30 minutes or until golden brown and cooked through.

barley, bean and vegetable soup

SERVES 4

115 g (4 oz/½ cup) barley

2 tablespoons olive oil

1 onion, diced

2 zucchini (courgettes), diced

2 red-skinned potatoes, peeled and diced

2 garlic cloves, crushed

700 g (1 lb 9 oz) silverbeet (swiss chard), finely shredded

1 litre (35 fl oz/4 cups) chicken or vegetable stock

400 g (14 oz) tin cannellini beans, rinsed

200 g (7 oz) green beans, topped and cut into short lengths

85 g (3 oz/½ cup) peas (fresh or frozen)

sea salt

freshly ground black pepper

to serve

parmesan cheese

Put the barley in a large saucepan, cover with cold water and bring to the boil. Reduce the heat and simmer for 45 minutes, or until the barley is tender. Rinse under cold running water, drain well and set aside.

Heat the olive oil in a large heavy-based saucepan over medium heat. Add the onion and cook, stirring occasionally, for 5 minutes. Add the zucchini, potato, garlic and silverbeet and cook, stirring occasionally, for 5 minutes more until the silverbeet has wilted.

Add the stock and 1 litre (35 fl oz/4 cups) of water and bring to the boil. Reduce the heat to low and simmer for 20 minutes. Add the cannellini beans and simmer for another 20 minutes. Add the barley, beans and peas and simmer for 5–10 minutes until the vegetables are tender. Season with the salt and pepper and grate parmesan cheese over the top to serve.

chickpea, burghul and parsley salad with marinated lamb

SERVES 4

3 tablespoons olive oil

2 teaspoons garam masala

400 g (14 oz) lamb backstrap

sea salt

freshly ground black pepper

200 g (7 oz) coarse burghul (bulgur)

400 g (14 oz) tin chickpeas, rinsed

2 fresh green chillies, finely chopped

8 spring onions (scallions), thinly sliced

large handful frsh flat-leaf (Italian) parsley, roughly chopped

1 garlic clove, crushed

3 tablespoons lemon juice

2 tablespoons pomegranate molasses

Mix 1 tablespoon of the olive oil with the garam masala. Brush all over the lamb, season with the salt and pepper and set aside for 30 minutes.

Put the burghul in a bowl, cover with hot water and leave to stand for 15 minutes. Drain the burghul, pressing out as much water as possible.

Put the burghul, chickpeas, chilli, spring onions and parsley in a bowl and stir together. Cover with plastic wrap and refrigerate. Stir together the garlic, lemon juice, pomegranate molasses, remaining olive oil, salt and pepper to make a dressing.

Preheat the oven to 180°C (350°F/Gas 4). Heat a large frying pan over medium-high heat and cook the lamb for 2 minutes on each side, or until browned. Transfer to a roasting tine and roast the lamb for 6–7 minutes (for medium). Leave for 10 minutes before carving into thin slices. Drizzle the dressing over the salad and serve with the lamb.

Pomegranate molasses is available from Middle Eastern food stores and speciality food stores.

spicy chicken thighs with cucumber and cashew salad

SERVES 4

3 tablespoons fish sauce
freshly ground black pepper
3 garlic cloves, crushed
2 large fresh red chillies, finely minced
2 teaspoons sugar
8 boneless, skinless chicken thighs
2 tablespoons vegetable oil

cucumber and cashew salad
3 tablespoons lime juice
3 tablespoons caster (superfine) sugar
200 g (7 oz) vermicelli noodles
2 cucumbers, halved and thinly sliced
small handful of fresh mint
4 spring onions (scallions), thinly sliced
2 tablespoons cashew nuts, crushed

Whisk the fish sauce, pepper, garlic, chilli and sugar in a bowl. Put the chicken in a separate bowl and pour over half the marinade. Cover with plastic wrap and refrigerate for 20 minutes (keep the rest of the marinade on one side).

Heat the oil in a large frying pan over medium-high heat. Add the chicken, in two batches, and cook for 3 minutes on each side, or until it is cooked through. (Sometimes I put another frying pan on top of the chicken and weigh it down with a couple of tins to make the chicken really crisp.)

While the chicken is cooking, add the lime juice and sugar to the marinade that you set aside. Stir until the sugar has dissolved to make a dressing.

Pour boiling water over the vermicelli and leave for a minute or so until soft. Drain under cold water, place in a large bowl and add the cucumber, mint, spring onions and cashews. Add the dressing, toss well and serve with the sliced chicken.

129

afternoon tea

As much as fashions change in food, baking is a true constant. Everyone who knows me knows how I love teatime with scones and teacakes, fancy sandwiches and a great smell wafting from the oven. In this hectic world I think it's something we should all enjoy as often as we can.

Even with simple food, afternoon teas feel luxurious. They're a celebration of the home-made in an era of mass production and they're special because they indicate that you're giving time to people you care about. Many of the things I serve for afternoon tea are classics, and they are classics simply because they're good. There's something very honest about baking at home.

I want my family to grow up with good memories around food. A freshly brewed cup of tea with a slice of cake still warm from the oven or a tart made from freshly picked apricots will become part of a happy memory. In fact, nothing makes me happier than filling the house with the warm aroma of freshly baked cakes.

choc banana bread

250 g (9 oz/2 cups) plain (all-purpose) flour

2 teaspoons baking powder

125 g (4½ oz) unsalted butter, softened

230 g (8¼ oz/1 cup) caster (superfine) sugar

4 ripe bananas, mashed

2 eggs, lightly beaten

1 teaspoon natural vanilla extract

170 g (6 oz/1 cup) good-quality dark or milk chocolate chips

to serve

butter

Preheat the oven to 180°C (350°F/Gas 4). Sift the flour and baking powder into a large bowl.

Mix the butter, sugar, banana, eggs, vanilla and chocolate chips in a separate bowl. Add to the dry ingredients and stir to combine, being careful not to overmix.

Pour the batter into a non-stick, or lightly greased and floured, 19 × 11 cm (7½ × 4¼ inch) loaf (bar) tin and bake for 1 hour 15 minutes, or until the bread is cooked when tested with a skewer. Leave to cool in the tin for 5 minutes before turning out onto a wire rack to cool. Serve in thick slices with butter.

When mixing batters, you will often see the words 'do not overmix'. This is so you don't work the gluten in the flour and toughen the mixture as this makes the end result tough and dry. A loose mixture ensures a moist and delicious result.

plum and vanilla cake

SERVES 10 TO 12

topping
90 g (3¼ oz) plain (all-purpose) flour
100 g (3½ oz) unsalted butter, chopped
into small pieces
80 g (3¼ oz/⅓ cup) caster (superfine)
sugar

cake
180 g (6¼ oz) unsalted butter, softened
230 g (8¼ oz/1 cup) caster (superfine)
sugar
3 eggs, lightly beaten
1 teaspoon natural vanilla extract
185 g (6½ oz/1½ cups) plain (all-purpose)
flour
2 teaspoons baking powder
500 g (1 lb 2 oz) fresh plums, halved and
stoned, or 825 g (1 lb 13 oz) tinned
plums, stoned

to serve
pouring (whipping) cream

Preheat the oven to 180°C (350°F/Gas 4). To make the topping, place the flour, butter and sugar in a bowl and rub with your fingertips until crumbly (this can be done in a food processor if you prefer).

To make the cake, cream the butter and sugar together in a bowl until light and fluffy. Add the eggs, one at a time, beating well after each addition. Mix in the vanilla. Sift the flour and baking powder into the bowl and fold into the mixture. Spread into a 24 cm (9 inch) greased or non-stick springform cake tin. Top with halved plums with the cut side up. Sprinkle with the topping and bake for 1 hour, or until a skewer inserted into the centre of the cake comes out clean.

Remove from the oven and allow to cool in the tin for 10 minutes. Delicious served with pouring cream.

simple scones

1 tablespoon icing (confectioners') sugar

310 g (11 oz/2½ cups) plain (all-purpose) flour

1½ teaspoons baking powder

a pinch of salt

250 ml (9 fl oz/1 cup) milk

30 g (1 oz) butter, melted

to serve

jam

lightly whipped cream

Preheat the oven to 220°C (425°F/Gas 7). Sift the icing sugar, flour, baking powder and salt into a bowl. Add the milk and butter and stir to combine with a knife. Knead quickly and lightly until smooth and then press out to 3 cm (1¼ inch) deep on a floured surface.

Use a glass to cut out rounds roughly 5 cm (2 inch) in diameter and 3 cm (1¼ inch) deep and place them close together on a greased baking tray. Gather the scraps together, lightly knead again, then cut out more rounds. Cook for 8–10 minutes, until puffed and golden. Serve with jam and lightly whipped cream.

When whipping cream, take care to not overwhip. The cream should be still quite soft and wet, not firm and dry.

coconut blackberry slice

base

125 g (4½ oz) unsalted butter

55 g (2 oz/¼ cup) caster (superfine) sugar

1 egg

1 teaspoon natural vanilla extract

185 g (6½ oz/1½ cups) plain (all-purpose) flour

1 teaspoon baking powder

60 ml (2 fl oz/¼ cup) milk

filling

160 g (5¾ oz/½ cup) blackberry jam

250 g (9 oz) blackberries

topping

100 g (3½ oz) unsalted butter

5 tablespoons caster (superfine) sugar

2 eggs

225 g (8 oz/2½ cups) desiccated coconut

60 g (2¼ oz/½ cup) plain (all-purpose) flour

Preheat the oven to 180°C (350°F/Gas 4). To make the base, cream the butter and sugar in a bowl until light and fluffy. Add the egg and vanilla and stir with a wooden spoon to combine. Sift the flour and baking powder over the butter mixture, add the milk, and stir to combine.

Flour your hands and press the base evenly into a 30 x 20 cm (12 x 8 inch) baking tin, greased and lined with baking paper. Spread the base evenly with jam and sprinkle with blackberries.

To make the topping, cream the butter and sugar in a bowl until light and fluffy. Add the eggs, one at a time, and beat until combined. Stir in the coconut and 1 tablespoon sifted flour, then stir in the remaining flour. Spread the topping evenly over the blackberries.

Bake the slice for 25 minutes, or until golden. Cover with foil and cook for another 10 minutes. Remove from the oven and allow to cool in the tin for 10 minutes. Remove from the tin, cut into rectangles and serve warm or at room temperature.

strawberry shortcakes

100 g (3½ oz) cold unsalted butter, cut into small pieces
250 g (9 oz/2 cups) plain (all-purpose) flour
55 g (2 oz/¼ cup) caster (superfine) sugar
1 tablespoon baking powder
a pinch of salt
125 ml (4 fl oz/½ cup) cream
1 egg
1 egg yolk, extra
1 tablespoon cream, extra
450 g (1 lb/3 cups) strawberries
90 g (3¼ oz/¼ cup) honey
1 tablespoon lemon juice

to serve
thick (double/heavy) cream
icing (confectioners') sugar, for sprinkling

Preheat the oven to 200°C (400°F/Gas 6). Process the pieces of butter with the flour, sugar, baking powder and salt in a food processor until the mixture resembles coarse breadcrumbs. Transfer to a large bowl.

Mix the cream and egg in a small bowl until combined, then add to the flour and butter mixture and fold in with a knife until just combined. Turn out the dough onto a lightly floured surface and pat out to 2.5 cm (1 inch) thick. Cut out six rounds with a 7 cm (2 ¾ inch) cutter. Place on a baking tray lined with baking paper.

Mix the extra egg yolk and cream and brush on top of the dough rounds. Bake for 20–25 minutes, or until lightly golden. Cool on wire racks for 15 minutes.

While the shortcakes are cooking, hull and slice the strawberries and put them in a bowl. Add the honey and lemon juice and stir to combine.

To serve, slice open each shortcake with a knife and place the bottom halves on a plate. Top each with double cream and strawberries, then replace the tops of the shortcakes. Sprinkle with icing sugar.

apricot slice

185 g (6½ oz/1½ cups) plain (all-purpose) flour
170 g (6 oz/¾ cup) caster (superfine) sugar
1 teaspoon baking powder
a pinch of salt
3 eggs
60 ml (2 fl oz/¼ cup) milk
2 teaspoons natural vanilla extract
180 g (6¼ oz) butter, softened
14 apricots, halved and stoned (this may vary depending on the size of the apricots)
2 tablespoons caster (superfine) sugar, extra

Preheat the oven to 160°C (315°F/Gas 2–3). Sift the flour, sugar, baking powder and salt into a large bowl and make a well in the centre. Place the eggs, milk and vanilla in another bowl and mix to combine. Pour the egg mixture and butter into the well in the dry ingredients and beat for 2 minutes until smooth. Spread the mixture evenly into a greased or non-stick 20 x 30 cm (8 x 12 inch) lamington tin.

Push the apricot halves, cut side up, evenly into the cake mixture in four rows of seven. Place in the oven and bake for 20 minutes, sprinkle over the extra sugar and cook for another 20 minutes, or until a skewer inserted into the centre comes out clean. To serve, cut into fingers with two apricot halves per slice.

If fresh apricots are out of season, you can use bottled or tinned ones.

coconut and lime macadamia cake

200 g (7 oz/1¼ cups) macadamia nuts
40 g (1½ oz/⅓ cup) self-raising flour
a pinch of salt
6 eggs, separated
165 g (5¾ oz/¾ cup) sugar
finely grated zest of 1 lime
45 g (1¾ oz/½ cup) desiccated coconut
lime icing (see below)

Preheat the oven to 180°C (350°F/Gas 4). Place the nuts, flour and salt in the bowl of a food processor and process until the nuts are ground. Place the egg yolks and sugar in a bowl and beat for 3 minutes, or until the mixture is pale and creamy. Fold through the zest and coconut then the nut mixture. Place the egg whites in a clean, dry stainless steel bowl and whisk until stiff peaks form. Using a large metal spoon, fold lightly through the nut batter.

Spread the batter evenly into a 23 cm (9 inch) greased or non-stick springform cake tin. Bake for 40 minutes, or until the cake is lightly golden.

Remove from the oven and leave to sit for 10 minutes in the tin. Turn the cake out onto a serving plate. Spread the lime icing over the warm cake, allowing it to drizzle down the sides.

LIME ICING

125 g (4½ oz/1 cup) icing (confectioners')
sugar, sifted
2 tablespoons lime juice
1 teaspoon finely grated lime zest

Combine all the ingredients in a bowl and mix until smooth and glossy.

vanilla cup cakes

MAKES 12

125 g (4½ oz) unsalted butter, softened

230 g (8¼ oz/1 cup) caster (superfine) sugar

1½ teaspoons natural vanilla extract

3 eggs

185 g (6½ oz/1½ cups) plain (all-purpose) flour

1 teaspoon baking powder

½ teaspoon salt

185 ml (6 fl oz/¾ cup) milk

icing (see below)

fresh raspberries, to decorate

Preheat the oven to 180°C (350°F/Gas 4). Line a 12-hole 125 ml (4 fl oz/½ cup) capacity muffin tray with paper cases. Place the butter and sugar in a bowl and beat until light and fluffy. Add the vanilla, then add the eggs, one at a time, beating well after each addition. Sift the flour, baking powder and salt and gradually fold into the mixture, alternating with the milk, until it has a soft dropping consistency. Spoon into the cases and bake for 20–25 minutes until golden. Remove from the oven and cool for 10 minutes in the tin. Turn the cakes out onto a wire rack to cool. Ice the cakes when cold and top with raspberries.

ICING

60 g (2¼ oz/½ cup) icing (confectioners') sugar, sifted

2–3 teaspoons hot water

a few drops of natural vanilla extract

Place all the ingredients in a bowl and mix until smooth.

mandarin chocolate cake

250 g (9 oz) good-quality dark chocolate, chopped into small pieces
250 g (9 oz) unsalted butter, chopped into small pieces
6 eggs, separated
115 g (4 oz/½ cup) caster (superfine) sugar
3 tablespoons plain (all-purpose) flour, sifted
25 g (1 oz/¼ cup) ground almonds
1 tablespoon mandarin zest (if mandarins are out of season, use oranges or tangerines)

to serve
cocoa powder, for dusting
mandarin slices
lightly whipped cream

Preheat the oven to 190°C (375°F/Gas 5). Place the chocolate and butter in a heatproof bowl over a saucepan of simmering water, making sure the bowl does not touch the water. Stir the chocolate and butter over the heat until just melted, being careful not to overheat. Remove from the heat and set aside.

Place the egg yolks and sugar in a bowl and mix until lightly combined. Gradually add the melted chocolate to the egg mixture, stirring constantly. Using a large metal spoon, fold through the flour, ground almonds and mandarin zest.

Place the egg whites in a clean, dry stainless steel bowl and whisk until stiff peaks form. Using a large metal spoon, fold half of the egg whites lightly through the batter until barely combined. Fold through the remaining egg whites, again barely combining.

Pour the batter into a 23 cm (9 inch) greased or non-stick springform cake tin and bake for 35 minutes. Don't worry if the cake still seems to be very wet in the centre: it will firm up a little on cooling.

Remove the cake from the oven and leave to cool completely in the tin. Transfer to a serving platter and dust with the cocoa powder. Serve with the mandarin slices and lightly whipped cream.

banana maple upside-down cake

SERVES 10 TO 12

50 g (1¾ oz) unsalted butter

55 g (2 oz/¼ cup) soft brown sugar

60 ml (2 fl oz/¼ cup) maple syrup

3–4 bananas, peeled and sliced in half lengthways

100 g (3½ oz) unsalted butter, softened, extra

230 g (8¼ oz/1 cup) caster (superfine) sugar

4 eggs

1 teaspoon natural vanilla extract

155 g (5½ oz/1¼ cup) plain (all-purpose) flour

1 teaspoon baking powder

a pinch of salt

to serve

vanilla ice cream (optional)

Preheat the oven to 180°C (350°F/Gas 4). To make the topping, place the butter, brown sugar and maple syrup in a small saucepan. Cook over a medium heat for 10 minutes, or until the sugar melts and the syrup is rich and golden. Pour the syrup into a 23 cm (9 inch) greased or non-stick springform cake tin and arrange the sliced bananas, cut side down, over the base of the tin.

To make the cake, place the extra butter and caster sugar in a bowl and beat until pale and creamy. Add the eggs one at a time, beating after each addition, then add the vanilla.

Sift the flour, baking powder and salt and gently fold through the mixture. Spoon the batter evenly over the bananas and caramel and smooth the top with a spatula.

Place the cake in the oven on a baking tray to catch any escaping caramel and bake for 35 minutes, or until a skewer inserted into the centre of the cake comes out clean.

Remove from the oven and leave in the tin for 5 minutes to cool slightly. Transfer to a large serving plate. Serve warm with vanilla ice cream, if desired.

This recipe can also be made very successfully with granny smith apples. Cook the sliced apples in the caramel for 5 minutes before placing in the tin and topping with the cake mixture.

friands

135 g (4¾ oz/1⅓ cups) ground almonds
220 g (7¾ oz/1¾ cups) icing (confectioners')
sugar, sifted
85 g (3 oz/⅔ cup) plain (all-purpose) flour,
sifted
8 egg whites
150 g (5½ oz) unsalted butter, melted
210 g (7½ oz/1½ cups) cherries or
115 g (4 oz/1 cup) raspberries or
3 nectarines, chopped
icing (confectioners') sugar, extra, for
dusting

Preheat the oven to 180°C (350°F/Gas 4). Grease and flour a non-stick 12-hole friand tin. Mix together the ground almonds, icing sugar and flour. Stir in the egg whites until just combined. Stir in the melted butter.

Pour the batter into the tins. Pit the cherries and cut in half. Arrange a few cherry halves or raspberries or nectarine pieces on top of each friand.

Bake for 25–30 minutes or until pale and golden. The friands should spring back when touched. Remove from the oven and leave in the tin for 5 minutes before turning out onto a wire rack to cool. Dust with extra icing sugar and store in an airtight container.

buttermilk cake with raspberry syrup

SERVES 8 TO 10

125 g (4½ oz) unsalted butter, softened

230 g (8¼ oz/1 cup) caster (superfine) sugar

2 eggs

250 ml (9 fl oz/1 cup) buttermilk

1 teaspoon natural vanilla extract

250 g (9 oz/2 cups) plain (all-purpose) flour

2 teaspoons baking powder

a pinch of salt

raspberry syrup (see below)

to serve

lightly whipped cream

raspberries

Preheat the oven to 180°C (350°F/Gas 4). Using electric beaters, cream the butter and sugar until pale and fluffy. Add the eggs, one at a time, beating well after each addition. With the mixer at low speed, beat in the buttermilk and the vanilla until just combined. Sift in the flour, baking powder and salt in two batches, mixing well after each addition.

Spoon the mixture into a 20 cm (8 inch) cake tin, greased and lined with baking paper, and smooth the top. Bake for 45–50 minutes, or until a skewer comes out clean. Leave to cool in the tin for 10 minutes, then transfer to a plate and pour syrup over the top.

Place slices of cake on serving plates with some lightly whipped cream and raspberries.

RASPBERRY SYRUP

110 g (3¾ oz/½ cup) sugar

2 tablespoons lemon juice

220 g (7¾ oz) raspberries

Stir the sugar, lemon juice and ¼ cup 60 ml (2 fl oz/¼ cup) water in a saucepan over a medium to high heat until the sugar dissolves. Cook for 2–3 minutes, then add the raspberries and lightly crush with the back of a spoon. Cook for another 3 minutes, then remove from the heat and purée in a blender.

coconut macaroons

MAKES 20

2 egg whites
115 g (4 oz/½ cup) caster (superfine) sugar
120 g (4½ oz/2 cups) shredded coconut
100 g (3½ oz/¾ cup) roughly chopped
macadamia nuts
1 teaspoon lime zest

Preheat the oven to 160°C (315°F/Gas 2–3). Mix together the egg whites, sugar, coconut, nuts and lime zest in a bowl (you may need to use your hands).

Shape tablespoons of the mixture into mounds on baking trays lined with baking paper. Bake for 10–15 minutes or until light golden brown. Cool on the trays.

I sometimes serve coconut macaroons as a dessert with a scoop of coconut ice cream.

apricot bars

155 g (5½ oz/1¼ cups) plain (all-purpose) flour
95 g (3¼ oz/½ cup) soft brown sugar
115 g (4 oz/½ cup) caster (superfine) sugar
2 pinches of salt
1 teaspoon baking powder
175 g (6 oz) unsalted butter, chilled and diced
130 g (4¾ oz/1 cup) rolled (porridge) oats
90 g (3¼ oz/1 cup) desiccated coconut
450 g (1 lb/2½ cups) dried apricots, chopped
100 g (3½ oz/⅓ cup) apricot jam
40 g (1½ oz) unsalted butter, extra, melted

Preheat the oven to 180°C (350°F/Gas 4). Mix the flour, sugars, salt, baking powder and butter in a food processor until a dough forms. (Or, rub the ingredients together with your fingertips.) Mix in the oats and coconut. Reserve a cupful of dough and press the remainder evenly into a 20 x 30 cm (8 x 12 inch) baking tin, lightly greased and lined with baking paper. Bake for 15 minutes, or until golden.

Put the apricots and 125 ml (4 fl oz/½ cup) of water in a small saucepan over low heat and cook, stirring occasionally, until the liquid has been absorbed. Cool slightly, then spoon over the dough base. Dot the jam over the apricots and crumble the reserved dough over the top. Spoon on the melted butter and bake for 30–35 minutes until lightly golden. Leave to cool completely in the tray. Slice into squares and store in an airtight container.

peach and raspberry slice

185 g (6½ oz/1½ cups) plain
(all-purpose) flour
1½ teaspoons baking powder, plus
½ teaspoon extra
125 g (4½ oz) butter, chilled and diced
115 g (4 oz/½ cup) soft brown sugar
115 g (4 oz/½ cup) caster (superfine) sugar
3 ripe peaches, peeled and sliced into
wedges (see below)
90 g (3¼ oz/¾ cup) raspberries, fresh
or frozen
2 teaspoons natural vanilla extract
1 egg, lightly beaten
185 ml (6 fl oz/¾ cup) milk

Preheat the oven to 180°C (350°F/Gas 4). Grease and line the base of a 20 x 30 cm (8 x 12 inch) baking tin with baking paper. Sift the flour and baking powder into a large bowl and then rub in the butter with your fingertips. Stir in both the sugars. Press half the mixture over the base of the tin. Lay the peaches over the top and sprinkle with raspberries.

Add the vanilla, extra baking powder, egg and milk to the rest of the base mixture and stir well – don't worry too much about lumps. Pour evenly over the top of the peaches and raspberries and bake for 1 hour. Cool in the tray, then cut into squares to serve.

To peel peaches, score a cross in the skin with a sharp knife, then blanch the peaches in boiling water for 30 seconds, refresh in cold water and peel the skin away from the cross.

lamingtons

sponge cake

6 eggs

150 g (5½ oz/⅔ cup) caster (superfine) sugar

200 g (7 oz/1⅔ cups) self-raising flour

30 g (1 oz) unsalted butter, melted

chocolate icing

500 g (1 lb 2 oz/4 cups) icing (confectioners') sugar

200 g (7 oz/1⅓ cups) dark chocolate, chopped

15 g (½ oz) unsalted butter

125 ml (4 fl oz/½ cup) milk

360 g (12¾ oz/4 cups) desiccated coconut

Preheat the oven to 180°C (350°F/Gas 4). Lightly grease and line the base of an 18 x 28 cm (7 x 11¼ inch) baking tin with baking paper.

To make the cake, whisk the eggs for about 5 minutes with an electric mixer until light and fluffy. Gradually add the sugar and continue beating until the mixture is thick and the sugar has dissolved. Sift over the flour and fold in lightly. Add the butter and 3 tablespoons of hot water and stir gently to combine. Pour into the tin and bake for 30 minutes, or until golden. Cool on a wire rack.

To make the chocolate icing, put the sugar, dark chocolate, butter and milk in a heatproof bowl and place over a saucepan of simmering water. Stir constantly until melted and combined.

Cut the sponge into 16 squares. Put the coconut in a bowl. Dip each sponge square into the chocolate icing and then in the coconut. Leave on a wire rack to dry completely before serving.

fresh apricot and cinnamon cake

SERVES 8

140 g (5 oz) self-raising flour

½ teaspoon ground cinnamon

50 g (1¾ oz/¼ cup) caster (superfine) sugar

1 egg, lightly beaten

3 tablespoons milk

1 teaspoon natural vanilla extract

85 g (3 oz) unsalted butter, melted

350 g (12 oz) fresh apricots, halved and stoned

topping

40 g (1½ oz/⅓ cup) plain (all-purpose) flour

1 teaspoon ground cinnamon

35 g (1¼ oz) caster (superfine) sugar

35 g (1¼ oz) unsalted butter, chilled and diced

Preheat the oven to 180°C (350°F/Gas 4). Grease and line the base of a 20 cm (8 inch) round spring-form cake tin with baking paper. Sift the flour and cinnamon into a large bowl and stir in the sugar. Make a well in the centre and pour in the egg, milk, vanilla and melted butter. Mix with a wooden spoon until the batter is smooth, then spoon into the tin. Arrange the apricots, cut side up, evenly over the batter and then gently press them down.

For the topping, put the flour, cinnamon and sugar in a bowl. Rub in the butter with your fingertips until crumbs form. Scatter the topping evenly over the apricots.

Bake for 35–40 minutes, or until the cake is light golden and a skewer inserted into the centre comes out clean. Leave to cool in the tin for 10 minutes before transferring to a wire rack to cool completely.

almond and raspberry slice

topping
60 g (2½ oz) unsalted butter, softened
55 g (2 oz/¼ cup) caster (superfine) sugar
1 teaspoon natural vanilla extract
200 g (7 oz) flaked almonds
2 tablespoons milk

base
150 g (5½ oz) unsalted butter, softened
110 g (3¾ oz/½ cup) caster
(superfine) sugar
1 teaspoon natural vanilla extract
225 g (8 oz/1¾ cups) plain
(all-purpose) flour
40 g (1½ oz/⅓ cup) cornflour (cornstarch)

filling
160 g (5¾ oz/½ cup) raspberry jam

Preheat the oven to 180°C (350°F/Gas 4). Lightly grease a
24 × 20 cm (9½ × 8 inch) baking tin and line with baking paper.

To make the almond topping, put the butter, sugar, vanilla, almonds
and milk in a saucepan. Cook over a very low heat until the butter
has melted, then leave to cool.

To make the base, beat the butter, sugar and vanilla with electric
beaters until pale and creamy. Sift the flour and cornflour together
and add in two batches, beating on low speed until just mixed.
Press the dough into the baking tin and bake for 12 minutes, or
until light golden. Remove from the oven and leave to cool for
10 minutes.

Carefully spread the jam over the pastry base, then spread the
cooled almond topping over the jam. Return to the oven and bake
for a further 25 minutes, or until golden brown.

chocolate caramel slice

125 g (4½ oz/1 cup) plain
(all-purpose) flour
1 teaspoon baking powder
90 g (3¼ oz/1 cup) desiccated coconut
115 g (4 oz/½ cup) caster
(superfine) sugar
125 g (4½ oz) unsalted butter, melted

filling
100 g (3½ oz) unsalted butter
100 g (3½ oz) brown sugar
400 ml (14 fl oz) tin condensed milk
2 tablespoons golden syrup
1 teaspoon natural vanilla extract

topping
150 g (5½ oz) good-quality dark chocolate
1 teaspoon flaked sea salt, such as Maldon
sea salt

Preheat the oven to 180°C (350°F/Gas 4) and lightly grease and line an 18 x 28 cm (7 x 11¼ inch) baking tin with baking paper.

Sift the flour and baking powder into a large bowl, add the coconut, sugar and melted butter and stir together well. Press firmly into the base of the tin and bake for 12 minutes, or until light golden.

To make the filling, put the butter, brown sugar, condensed milk, golden syrup and vanilla in a saucepan over a low heat. Cook, stirring, until the sugar has dissolved. Bring to the boil, then reduce the heat to low and cook, stirring, for 5 minutes, or until light golden. Pour evenly over the cooked base, then return to the oven and bake for 10 minutes. Set aside to cool completely.

Once the caramel is cool, put the chocolate in a heatproof bowl over a saucepan of gently simmering water, stirring occasionally until the chocolate has melted (or melt the chocolate very carefully in a microwave oven). Spread the chocolate evenly over the caramel. Once the chocolate has set, sprinkle with the sea salt and cut into squares.

bill's biscuits

PISTACHIO BISCUITS

125 g (4½ oz) shelled pistachios
125 g (4½ oz) unsalted butter, softened
115 g (4 oz/½ cup) caster (superfine) sugar
I egg
I tablespoon rosewater
185 g (6½ oz/1½ cups) plain (all-purpose) flour, sifted
I teaspoon baking powder, sifted
2 tablespoons plain (all-purpose) flour, extra

Place the pistachios in a small bowl, cover with water and set aside for 30 minutes. (It is important to soak the pistachios so you can slice through them when cutting the dough.) Place the butter and sugar in a bowl and beat until pale and creamy. Add the egg and mix until combined. Add the rosewater, and stir until smooth. Drain the pistachios well then add to the batter with the flour and baking powder. Fold through until a stiff dough forms.

Sift the extra flour over a clean dry surface, and knead the dough lightly for 30 seconds. Divide the dough in half and roll each into a log, roughly 5 cm (2 inches) in diameter. Wrap each log in plastic wrap and refrigerate for 30 minutes.

Preheat the oven to 180°C (350°F/Gas 4). Remove the dough from the refrigerator, and slice into 5 mm (¼ inch) rounds. Place biscuits 2 cm (¾ inch) apart on a baking tray lined with baking paper. Bake for 10–12 minutes, or until lightly golden. Remove from the oven and leave to cool on a wire rack.

ORANGE AND CARDAMOM BISCUITS

375 g (13 oz/3 cups) plain (all-purpose) flour
2 teaspoons baking powder
I tablespoon ground ginger
I teaspoon ground nutmeg
I teaspoon ground cardamom
250 g (9 oz) unsalted butter, softened
345 g (12 oz/1½ cups) soft brown sugar
3 teaspoons brandy
finely grated zest of I orange
30 g (1 oz/¼ cup) plain (all-purpose) flour, extra
I egg white, for glazing
30 g (1 oz) granulated sugar

Sift the flour, baking powder, ginger, nutmeg and cardamom into a large bowl. Place the butter and brown sugar in a bowl and beat until pale and creamy. Add the brandy and zest and mix well. Using a large metal spoon, fold the dry ingredients through in two batches.

Sift the extra flour over a clean dry surface and knead the dough for 30 seconds. Roll the dough into a large rectangle 5 mm (¼ inch) thick. Cut into shapes 3 x 6 cm (1¼ x 2½ inches) long. Brush with the egg white and sprinkle with sugar.

Preheat the oven to 180°C (350°F/Gas 4). Place the biscuits 2 cm (¾ inch) apart on a baking tray lined with baking paper. Bake for 10–12 minutes, or until lightly browned. Remove from the oven and leave to cool on a wire rack.

175

dinner

The older I get the more simply I like to eat and the more I appreciate uncomplicated things. But, if I have time, I enjoy making a complicated dinner with the day spent shopping and cooking something challenging. I also love an appreciative audience when cooking. Having said that, I'm not hugely in favour of formal dinners and I rarely serve a three-course, sit-down meal.

I love it when I'm invited to someone else's house for dinner, but I don't get asked that often. I suspect people are afraid of what I might think of their cooking. If only they knew it's not the food that makes or breaks an occasion. Being a good host is about enjoying yourself as well as entertaining others.

I often get asked what makes a great dinner party and I think the best advice I can give is very simple. Be realistic about your time (everything will always take longer than you think) and invite the right mix of people. I've met most of my closest friends over a dinner table.

mushroom soup

350 g (12 oz) button mushrooms
250 g (9 oz) potatoes, peeled and
roughly chopped
25 g (1 oz) butter
2 tablespoons olive oil
2 garlic cloves, finely chopped
sea salt
freshly ground black pepper
125 ml (4 fl oz/½ cup) dry white wine
2 teaspoons finely chopped fresh oregano
1.5 litres (52 fl oz/6 cups) chicken stock
or water

to serve
fresh parsley sprigs
4 tablespoons sour cream (optional)

Finely chop the mushrooms in a food processor using the pulse action. Remove and repeat the process with the potatoes.

Heat the butter and oil in a large saucepan over a medium heat. Add the mushrooms, garlic and a little salt and pepper, and cook for 10 minutes. Add the potato, wine, oregano and stock and bring to the boil over a high heat. Reduce the heat to low and simmer for 25 minutes. Let the soup cool slightly, then transfer 375 ml (13 fl oz/1½ cups) of the soup to a blender and blend until smooth. Return to the saucepan and stir well.

Ladle into serving bowls, top with a sprig of parsley and a tablespoon of sour cream, if you wish.

To change the flavour of this soup, just use different types of mushrooms. Darker ones will give a richer flavour, whereas lighter ones will give a more delicate flavour.

179

garlic prawns

20 raw king prawns (shrimp), peeled, deveined and tails left intact

250 ml (9 fl oz/1 cup) olive oil

5 garlic cloves, finely chopped

3 small fresh red chillies, split lengthways but intact at stem

1 teaspoon sea salt

freshly ground black pepper

2 tablespoons chopped fresh flat-leaf (Italian) parsley

to serve

lemon wedges

crusty bread

green salad

Preheat the oven to 250°C (500°F/Gas 9). Cut a slit down the back of each prawn and place the prawns in an ovenproof dish that will hold them snugly in a single layer.

Heat the oil in a large ovenproof frying pan over a high heat. Add half the garlic and all the chillies and cook for 1 minute or until the garlic starts to change colour. Pour over the prawns, then sprinkle with the remaining garlic. Season with the salt and pepper, cover with foil and bake for 10 minutes, or until the prawns are pink and cooked through. Don't overcook — remember that the prawns will continue cooking after being removed from the oven. Serve in a large bowl or divide among four serving dishes. Sprinkle with parsley and serve with lemon wedges, crusty bread and a green salad.

spaghetti with spicy meatballs

80 ml (2½ fl oz/⅓ cup) milk

1 slice of bread, crust removed

500 g (1 lb 2 oz) minced (ground) beef, or pork and veal

1 small onion, finely chopped

2 tablespoons fresh flat-leaf (Italian) parsley, chopped

1 teaspoon fresh thyme, finely chopped

1 egg, lightly beaten

25 g (1 oz/¼ cup) freshly grated parmesan cheese

2 garlic cloves, finely crushed

2 fresh red chillies, finely chopped

sea salt

freshly ground black pepper

60 ml (2 fl oz/¼ cup) olive oil

2 x 400 g (14 oz) tins chopped tomatoes

25 g (1 oz/½ cup) fresh basil leaves, shredded

500 g (1 lb 2 oz) spaghetti

to serve

a handful of fresh basil leaves, extra

freshly grated parmesan cheese

Put the milk and bread in a small saucepan and place over a low heat. When the bread has absorbed the milk, remove from the heat and mash with a fork. Allow to cool.

Combine the meat, onion, parsley, thyme, egg, parmesan, garlic, half of the chilli, the bread mixture and lots of salt and pepper in a large bowl. Gently mix with your hands, then shape into small balls. I find wetting my hands makes this easier.

Heat the oil in a large frying pan over a medium heat and, when hot, add the meatballs. Brown the meatballs on all sides, turning carefully. Alternatively, you can toss the meatballs in oil in a roasting tin and bake them at 220°C (425°F/Gas 7) for 10–15 minutes. You may find this easier because the meatballs won't break up. Drain off any excess oil (if you've baked the meatballs, transfer them to a frying pan) and add the tomatoes, remaining chilli, basil and salt and pepper. Stir the meatballs carefully to coat with the tomatoes, then simmer for 20 minutes.

While the meatballs are cooking, cook the pasta in a large pot of rapidly boiling salted water until *al dente*. Drain well.

To serve, divide the drained spaghetti among four bowls and spoon over the meatballs and sauce. Sprinkle with extra basil leaves and serve with freshly grated parmesan cheese.

rare roast beef fillet with roasted tomatoes and mustard cream

SERVES 4

1.5 kg (3 lb 5 oz) centre-cut beef fillet
sea salt
freshly ground black pepper
2 tablespoons olive oil
250 g (9 oz/1 bunch) watercress

to serve
roasted tomatoes (see below)
mustard cream (see below)
mashed potatoes

Preheat the oven to 240°C (475°F/Gas 8). Season the beef fillet with salt and pepper. Heat a large frying pan over a high heat and add the oil. When very hot, sear the beef on all sides until browned, then transfer to a roasting tin. Roast the beef, allowing 7 minutes per 500 g (1 lb 2 oz) for rare, and 10 minutes per 500 g (1 lb 2 oz) for medium. Remove from the oven and allow to rest in a warm place, covered with foil, for 7 minutes.

Pick the leaves off the watercress and discard the stalks. Cut the meat into thick slices and serve with the watercress, roasted tomatoes and some mashed potatoes. Drizzle with pan juices and serve with mustard cream.

ROASTED TOMATOES

4 ripe tomatoes, halved lengthways
sea salt
freshly ground black pepper
2 garlic cloves, finely sliced
20 g (¾ oz/¼ cup) fresh breadcrumbs
2 tablespoons fresh flat-leaf (Italian) parsley, finely chopped
2 tablespoons extra virgin olive oil

Preheat the oven to 200°C (400°F/Gas 6). Arrange the tomatoes with the cut sides up in a small roasting tin. Season with salt and pepper and sprinkle with garlic slices. Stir the breadcrumbs and parsley together in a bowl. Scatter over the tomatoes and drizzle with olive oil, then cook for 45 minutes.

MUSTARD CREAM

1 tablespoon dijon mustard
125 g (4½ oz/½ cup) crème fraîche or sour cream
1 teaspoon lemon juice
sea salt
freshly ground black pepper

Place all the ingredients in a bowl and stir to combine.

baked risotto with zucchini, tomato and parmesan

SERVES 4

2 tablespoons extra virgin olive oil
I onion, finely chopped
I teaspoon sea salt
220 g (7¾ oz/I cup) arborio rice
375 ml (13 fl oz/1½ cups) chicken stock or water
400 g (14 oz) tin chopped tomatoes
3 zucchini (courgettes), thinly sliced
60 g (2¼ oz) freshly grated parmesan cheese
freshly ground black pepper
2 tablespoons finely chopped fresh flat-leaf (Italian) parsley
shavings of parmesan cheese, for serving (optional)

Preheat the oven to 200°C (400°F/Gas 6). Heat a 3 litre (105 fl oz/12 cup) capacity flameproof casserole dish (with a lid) over a medium heat. Add the olive oil, onion and salt and stir for 5 minutes, or until the onion is soft and translucent.

Add the rice to the dish and stir for another minute. Add the stock or water and the chopped tomatoes and bring to simmering point. Stir in the zucchini and sprinkle with parmesan cheese and black pepper. Cover the dish and bake the risotto for 30 minutes, or until the rice is cooked. Scatter parsley over the top, sprinkle with parmesan shavings, if desired.

You can use this risotto as a base for other flavours — try replacing the zucchini with tinned tuna, or even a mixture of seafood. When using seafood I like to omit the parmesan cheese.

linguine with clams and tomatoes

SERVES 4 TO 6

400 g (14 oz) good-quality Italian dried linguine

60 ml (2 fl oz/¼ cup) extra virgin olive oil

3 garlic cloves, thinly sliced

2 small fresh red chillies, finely chopped, or ½ teaspoon dried chilli flakes

sea salt

1 kg (2 lb 4 oz) clams (vongole)

125 ml (4 fl oz/½ cup) white wine

500 g (1 lb 2 oz) cherry tomatoes, cut into halves

3 tablespoons fresh parsley, finely chopped

freshly ground black pepper

Cook the linguine in a large saucepan of rapidly boiling salted water until *al dente*.

While the pasta is cooking, heat the olive oil in a large deep frying pan over a medium heat.

Add the garlic, chilli and salt and cook gently for 1 minute. Add the clams, white wine and tomatoes. Cover the pan and cook for 3 minutes, or until the clams open. Discard any unopened clams. Remove from the heat.

Drain the pasta and add to the frying pan with the parsley. Gently toss to combine, then season with salt and pepper, to taste.

To get clams to spit out any grit they might have hidden in their shells, put them in a bowl of cold water with some oats or polenta. Rinse well before use.

baked polenta with a simple tomato sauce

SERVES 4

1 tablespoon sea salt
225 g (8 oz/1½ cups) instant polenta
1 tablespoon extra virgin olive oil
simple tomato sauce (see below)
350 g (12 oz) ricotta cheese
25 g (1 oz/¼ cup) finely grated parmesan cheese
freshly ground black pepper

Put 1.5 litres (52 fl oz/6 cups) water in a large saucepan over a high heat and bring to the boil. Add the salt and pour the polenta, constantly stirring with a wooden spoon, into the water in a steady stream. Reduce the heat to low, cover and cook for another 10 minutes, stirring regularly.

Lightly oil a 30 x 20 cm (12 x 8 inch) baking dish with half the olive oil. Pour the cooked polenta into the prepared dish and spread evenly. Leave to cool and firm in the baking dish then turn out onto a cutting board. Cut the polenta into 5 cm (2 inch) squares.

Preheat the oven to 200°C (400°F/Gas 6). Lightly grease a 20 x 25 cm (8 x 10 inch) gratin dish or four individual dishes with the remaining oil. Place the polenta squares in a single layer, slightly overlapping. Pour the simple tomato sauce evenly over the polenta. Crumble the ricotta and sprinkle parmesan cheese over the top. Season with pepper. Bake for 30 minutes, or until golden.

SIMPLE TOMATO SAUCE

2 x 400 g (14 oz) tins chopped tomatoes
2 tablespoons extra virgin olive oil
1 teaspoon sea salt
1 teaspoon sugar
freshly ground black pepper
2 garlic cloves, crushed

Place the tomatoes in a saucepan over a medium heat and cook for 15 minutes, stirring occasionally. Add the remaining ingredients, cook for 1 minute then remove from the heat.

Polenta is thick and sticky and needs to be stirred regularly so it doesn't catch on the base of the pan.

stir-fried mussels with chilli and blackbean

2 teaspoons sugar

2 tablespoons soy sauce

3 tablespoons shaoxing rice wine, or dry sherry

2 tablespoons vegetable oil

3 tablespoons fresh ginger, thinly sliced

4 spring onions (scallions), sliced into 5 cm (2 inch) lengths

4 garlic cloves, crushed

2 large fresh red chillies, halved lengthways

2 tablespoons fermented black beans, rinsed and crushed

1 kg (2 lb 4 oz) mussels, scrubbed and debearded

to serve
steamed rice

Place the sugar, soy sauce, shaoxing rice wine and 60 ml (2 fl oz/¼ cup) water in a small bowl and stir to combine. Heat a large wok or wide, flat saucepan until very hot, add the oil and when hot add the ginger, spring onion, garlic, chilli and black beans and stir for 30 seconds until aromatic. Add the mussels and toss to combine. Pour over the soy mixture, and cover. Cook covered for 2–5 minutes, shaking the pan, until the mussels open. Shake all the mussels, discarding any unopened ones, and sauce into a large warmed serving dish. Serve with steamed rice.

To prepare mussels, I scrub them under running water with a clean kitchen scourer which works marvellously to remove any residual seaweed or slime. Remove the beard. Discard any with broken shells and ones that don't close when tapped lightly on the bench.

lobster with lime butter

60 ml (2 fl oz/¼ cup) lime juice

125 g (4½ oz) butter, chopped

2 large raw lobster tails in the shell

sea salt

freshly ground black pepper

1 tablespoon olive oil

to serve

green bean salad (see below)

Place a baking tray in the oven and preheat to 220°C (425°F/Gas 7). To make the lime butter, heat the lime juice in a small saucepan over a medium heat. Add the butter and whisk constantly until melted. Set aside. Cut the lobster tails in half lengthways and season with salt and pepper. Place a large frying pan over a high heat, add the oil and arrange the lobsters cut side down in the pan. Sear for 2 minutes, place the lobsters on the hot baking tray, drizzle with lime butter and roast for 10–15 minutes, or until the lobster flesh is opaque and just cooked. Arrange the lobster tails on a platter and serve with green bean salad.

GREEN BEAN SALAD

500 g (1 lb 2 oz) green beans, topped

1 teaspoon wholegrain mustard

60 ml (2 fl oz/¼ cup) extra virgin olive oil

1 tablespoon red wine vinegar

sea salt

freshly ground black pepper

½ red onion, finely sliced

1 cup fresh flat-leaf (Italian) parsley,

Blanch the beans in boiling water for 2 minutes, or until just tender and bright green in colour. Drain and refresh under cold water.

Place the mustard, olive oil and vinegar in a large bowl and whisk to combine. Season with salt and pepper. Add the beans, onion and parsley and gently toss to combine.

caramel chicken

8 chicken thigh fillets, skinless, chopped in half

1 tablespoon vegetable oil

1 red onion, sliced

3 garlic cloves, sliced

freshly ground black pepper

60 ml (2 fl oz/¼ cup) dark soy sauce

115 g (4 fl oz/½ cup) soft brown sugar

60 ml (2 fl oz/¼ cup) fish sauce

to serve

steamed rice

steamed green vegetables, such as snow peas (mangetout), asparagus or Chinese broccoli (gai larn)

Place the chicken and oil in a bowl and toss to combine. Heat a large frying pan over a high heat until hot. Cook the chicken, in two batches, for 2 minutes on one side until lightly brown, turn and cook for another minute. Remove from the pan.

Reduce the heat to medium and add a little extra oil if needed. Add the onion and garlic and cook for 5 minutes, stirring occasionally. Return the chicken to the pan, sprinkle liberally with black pepper, add the soy sauce and stir to combine. Cover the pan, reduce heat to low and cook for 10 minutes, stirring occasionally. Increase the heat to high, add the sugar and stir to combine. Cook uncovered for 3–4 minutes, or until the sauce is rich, dark and syrupy and the chicken is cooked. Add the fish sauce and stir to combine. Place in a serving dish and serve with steamed rice and green vegetables.

marinated lamb with spicy eggplant salad

I teaspoon paprika

½ teaspoon ground cumin

2 garlic cloves, crushed

2 tablespoons olive oil

4 x 200 g (7 oz) lamb backstraps

sea salt

freshly ground black pepper

to serve

spicy eggplant salad (see below)

fresh coriander (cilantro) sprigs

plain yoghurt

Place the paprika, cumin, garlic and olive oil in a bowl and stir to combine. Trim the lamb of any excess fat and sinew then coat with the marinade. Cover with plastic wrap and place in the refrigerator to marinate for 2 hours, bringing to room temperature in the last 30 minutes.

Heat a frying pan over a high heat. Season the lamb with salt and pepper and cook for 3–4 minutes each side. Transfer the lamb to a plate, cover with foil and keep in a warm place for 10 minutes. Slice each lamb fillet on the diagonal into 2 cm (¾ inch) pieces and serve with the spicy eggplant salad, coriander sprigs and yoghurt.

SPICY EGGPLANT SALAD

2 large eggplants (aubergine)

2 tablespoons olive oil

3 garlic cloves, crushed

3 tablespoons fresh flat-leaf (Italian) parsley, chopped

3 tablespoons fresh coriander (cilantro) leaves, chopped

2 tablespoons paprika

I small fresh red chilli, seeded and finely chopped

½ teaspoon ground cumin

2 tablespoons olive oil, extra

4 large roma (plum) tomatoes, roughly chopped

I teaspoon sea salt

I tablespoon soft brown sugar

2 tablespoons lemon juice

I tablespoon red wine vinegar

freshly ground black pepper

Cut the eggplant into I cm (½ inch) thick slices. Preheat the oven to 200°C (400°F/Gas 6). Place the eggplant in a single layer on two baking trays and brush with olive oil on each side. Cook for 30 minutes, swapping the position of the trays halfway through. Remove from the oven. Sprinkle the eggplant with water if it is a little dry. Cool for 5 minutes, dice and place in a bowl. Add the garlic, parsley, coriander, paprika, chilli and cumin and stir to combine. Place the extra olive oil in a saucepan over a medium to high heat and add the tomatoes, salt and sugar. Cook for 10 minutes, add the eggplant mixture and cook for another 5 minutes. Remove from the heat and stir in the lemon juice, vinegar and pepper. Serve warm.

stuffed roast chicken

SERVES 4

6 thick slices good-quality bread (I like wholemeal (whole wheat))

1 tablespoon olive oil

155 g (5½ oz/1 cup) onion, roughly chopped

80 g (2¾ oz) pancetta, bacon or prosciutto, chopped

zest of 1 lemon, finely grated

1 tablespoon fresh sage or thyme, chopped

¼ cup fresh flat-leaf (italian) parsley, roughly chopped

sea salt

freshly ground black pepper

1 egg, lightly beaten

1 x 1.5 kg (3 lb 5 oz) free-range chicken

1 tablespoon olive oil, extra

to serve

roast vegetables (see below)

green salad (optional)

Preheat the oven to 220°C (425°F/Gas 7). Tear the bread roughly and place in a food processor and process until large breadcrumbs form. Place in a large bowl.

Place a frying pan over a medium heat. Put the olive oil in the pan, heat and add the onion. Cook for 3 minutes, stirring occasionally. Add the pancetta and cook for another 3 minutes. Remove the onion and pancetta and place in the bowl of breadcrumbs. Add the zest, sage, parsley, salt, pepper and egg and mix well to combine.

Wash the chicken and dry inside and out with paper towels. Fill the cavity with the stuffing mixture, then truss the chicken with kitchen string. Rub lightly with extra olive oil then season with salt and pepper.

Place the chicken in the oven, breast side up, and cook for 15 minutes. Lower the heat to 180°C (350°F/Gas 4) and cook for another hour, or until the juices run clear when a skewer is inserted into the thickest part of the thigh. Remove from the oven, loosely cover with foil and rest for 15 minutes before carving. Serve with a green salad, if desired, and the roast vegetables.

ROAST VEGETABLES

1 kg (2 lb 4 oz) pumpkin (winter squash), potato and sweet potato, cut into chunks

2 red onions, peeled and quartered

60 ml (2 fl oz/¼ cup) extra virgin olive oil

sea salt

freshly ground black pepper

Place all the ingredients in a bowl and toss to combine. Put into a baking dish, spreading the vegetables evenly, and bake at the same time as the chicken. Leave in the oven while the chicken is resting.

205

veal cutlets with tomatoes, capers and polenta

SERVES 4

4 large ripe tomatoes, each cut into
eight wedges

I tablespoon fresh oregano

2 tablespoons capers, rinsed and
squeezed dry

2 garlic cloves, sliced

I red onion, cut into fine wedges

2 tablespoons olive oil, plus extra for
brushing

sea salt

freshly ground black pepper

4 veal cutlets

to serve

polenta (see below)

I tablespoon salt

250 g (9 oz/1⅔ cups) polenta

50 g (1¾ oz/½ cup) freshly grated
parmesan cheese

Preheat the oven to 200°C (400°F/Gas 6). If you intend to serve these cutlets with polenta, start cooking your polenta now.

Put the tomatoes, oregano, capers, garlic, onion and olive oil in a small roasting tin (large enough to fit the veal cutlets) and toss together. Sprinkle with salt and pepper. Cover with foil and bake for 25–30 minutes. Remove the foil and bake for another 10 minutes.

While the tomatoes are cooking, brush the veal cutlets with oil and season liberally with salt and pepper. Heat a large frying pan over a high heat for 1–2 minutes, until very hot. Add the veal cutlets and cook for 1 minute on each side, or until the veal is sealed. Remove from the pan. Place the veal cutlets on top of the tomatoes and bake for 10–15 minutes, until the veal is cooked. Serve with polenta.

POLENTA

To make the polenta, you'll need a large heatproof bowl that will sit over a large saucepan. Fill the saucepan two-thirds with water but make sure the base of the bowl will not touch the water. Bring the water to the boil. Pour 1.75 litres (8 fl oz/7 cups) extra boiling water into the bowl, add the salt and polenta and whisk continuously for about 4 minutes, until the mixture thickens. Cover the bowl tightly with foil and sit the bowl over the saucepan of steadily boiling water. After 20 minutes, remove the bowl, carefully lift off the foil and thoroughly stir the polenta. Cover again and return to the heat. Do this every 20 minutes. Check the boiling water underneath as well, topping up as necessary. The polenta should be ready after it has cooked for 1½ hours. Stir in the parmesan cheese just before serving.

206

barbecued fish with preserved lemon dressing and parsley salad

SERVES 4

4 x 500 g (1 lb 2 oz) baby snappers, scaled
and cleaned
2 tablespoons olive oil
sea salt
freshly ground black pepper

to serve
preserved lemon dressing (see below)
parsley salad (see below)

60 ml (2 fl oz/¼ cup) extra virgin olive oil
freshly ground black pepper
1 tablespoon fresh oregano
3 tablespoons preserved lemon, rinsed
and thinly sliced

175 g (6 oz/1 cup) fine grain burghul (bulgur)
60 g (2¼ oz/½ cup) finely chopped spring
onions (scallions)
1 cup fresh flat-leaf (Italian) parsley, roughly
chopped
80 ml (2½ fl oz/⅓ cup) olive oil
60 ml (2 fl oz/¼ cup) lemon juice
1½ teaspoons ground cumin
1 fresh green chilli, seeded and finely chopped
2 Lebanese (short) cucumbers, quartered
lengthways and thinly sliced
sea salt
freshly ground black pepper

Make three diagonal slashes on both sides of each fish. Brush the fish with olive oil and season with salt and pepper. Heat the barbecue or grill (broiler) until very hot and cook for 4 minutes each side, or until the fish is opaque and just cooked. Remove the fish to a serving dish and drizzle over the preserved lemon dressing. Serve with the parsley salad.

PRESERVED LEMON DRESSING

Place the olive oil, 2 tablespoons water and pepper in a bowl and whisk to combine. Add the oregano and preserved lemon and stir to combine.

PARSLEY SALAD

Place the burghul in a fine sieve over the sink. Soak the burghul with lots of water, and let stand for 30 minutes. Squeeze out any remaining water before placing in a bowl with the remaining ingredients. Season to taste with salt and pepper then stir to combine.

grilled white fish with corn salsa

60 ml (2 fl oz/¼ cup) olive oil
1 teaspoon paprika
1 teaspoon ground cumin
4 x 200 g (7 oz) firm white fish fillets, such as blue-eye trevalla or snapper, skin removed
sea salt
freshly ground black pepper

to serve
fresh coriander (cilantro) sprigs, to garnish
corn salsa (see below)
lime cheeks

3 tablespoons olive oil
400 g (14 oz/2 cups) fresh corn kernels
200 g (7 oz) green beans, thinly sliced
sea salt
freshly ground black pepper
4 spring onions (scallions), finely chopped
½ cup fresh mint leaves, whole
1 fresh green chilli, chopped
2 tablespoons lime juice

Place the olive oil, paprika and cumin in a bowl and whisk to combine. Place the fish on a plate and pour over the marinade, turning the fish so it is evenly coated. Season with salt and pepper.

Heat a barbecue or grill (broiler) and cook the fish for 2–3 minutes. Turn and cook on the other side for 2–3 minutes, or until the fish is opaque and just cooked.

Garnish with coriander sprigs and serve on individual serving plates with the corn salsa and lime cheeks.

CORN SALSA

Place a frying pan over a medium to high heat and add the oil. Once the oil is hot, add the corn and beans. Season with salt and pepper and cook for 3 minutes. Place the spring onions, mint, chilli and lime juice in a bowl and add the corn mixture. Stir to combine.

marinated coriander chicken

2 small free-range chickens, around 1.2 kg (approximately 2 lb 11 oz) each, cut in half

2 cups fresh coriander (cilantro) stems and leaves, roughly chopped

2 teaspoons black peppercorns

2 teaspoons sea salt

3 garlic cloves

2 tablespoons lime juice

60 ml (2 fl oz/¼ cup) vegetable oil

to serve

fresh coriander (cilantro) sprigs

cucumber relish (see below)

lime cheeks

Soak eight wooden skewers in cold water for 30 minutes to stop them from burning during cooking. Wash the chicken and dry it with paper towels. Slash each chicken half a few times to allow the marinade flavours to penetrate. Run a wooden skewer through the flesh of each chicken piece to secure to the joints, and place in a large baking dish.

Place the coriander, peppercorns, salt, garlic, lime juice and oil in a blender or food processor and process until smooth. Pour the marinade over the chicken pieces, rubbing well into the flesh, and cover with plastic wrap. Place in the refrigerator to marinate for 2 hours, bringing to room temperature in the last 30 minutes.

Preheat the barbecue grill to high. Place the chicken halves on the barbecue and cook, cut side down, for 6–8 minutes. Turn and cook flesh side down for a further 5–6 minutes, or until the chicken is cooked through. Alternatively, preheat the oven to 220°C (425°F/ Gas 7). Place the chicken on a baking tray, skin side up, and bake for 30–35 minutes. Garnish with coriander sprigs and serve with the cucumber relish and lime cheeks.

CUCUMBER RELISH

125 ml (4 fl oz/½ cup) rice vinegar or white vinegar

115 g (4 oz/½ cup) caster (superfine) sugar

1 Lebanese (short) cucumber, quartered lengthways and thinly sliced

2 red Asian shallots or ½ red onion, thinly sliced

1 large fresh red chilli, seeded and thinly sliced

Place the vinegar and sugar in a small saucepan over a medium heat, and stir until the sugar has dissolved. Remove from the heat and cool. Pour into a bowl, add the cucumber, shallots and chilli and stir to combine.

marinated lamb cutlets with pilaff

SERVES 4

1 teaspoon crushed coriander seeds
1 teaspoon crushed fennel seeds
½ teaspoon ground cumin
¼ teaspoon dried chilli flakes
3 garlic cloves, sliced
3 tablespoons extra virgin olive oil
sea salt
freshly ground black pepper
12 French-trimmed lamb cutlets

to serve
warm lentil and rice pilaff (see below)
ginger tomato sauce (see below)
lemon wedges

185 g (6½ oz/1 cup) small green lentils
200 g (7 oz/1 cup) long-grain rice
½ lemon
2 tablespoons extra virgin olive oil
1 large onion, finely sliced
sea salt
freshly ground black pepper
½ cup fresh flat-leaf (Italian) parsley,
roughly chopped

Place all the ingredients except the lamb cutlets in a bowl and stir to combine. Add the lamb to the marinade and toss to coat. Cover with plastic wrap and place in the refrigerator to marinate for 2 hours, bringing to room temperature in the last 30 minutes.

Heat a frying pan over a high heat for 1 minute. Add the cutlets and cook for 1–2 minutes, turn and cook for another minute for medium-rare. Serve with the ginger tomato sauce, warm lentil and rice pilaff and lemon wedges.

WARM LENTIL AND RICE PILAFF
Bring a large pot of water to the boil, add the lentils and cook for 10 minutes. Add the rice and lemon and cook for another 12–15 minutes, or until the lentils and rice are tender. Drain, discarding the lemon, and place in a serving bowl.

Meanwhile, heat a frying pan over a medium to high heat. When hot, add the oil and onion, and cook for 10–12 minutes, or until the onion is a rich golden brown (don't worry if it catches a bit), stirring frequently. Remove from the heat. Sprinkle the pilaff with salt, pepper, parsley and half of the cooked onion. Stir to combine. Top with the remaining onion and serve.

GINGER TOMATO SAUCE
Make this simple ginger tomato sauce by frying a little chilli, ginger and garlic in olive oil until fragrant. Add 600 g (1 lb 5 oz) chopped tomatoes and cook for 25 minutes.

214

beef and mushroom pot pies with relish

SERVES 6

2 tablespoons plain (all-purpose) flour

2 teaspoons paprika

1 teaspoon sea salt

freshly ground black pepper

1.5 kg (3 lb 5 oz) chuck or blade steak, cut into 2 cm (¾ inch) chunks

400 g (14 oz) tin chopped tomatoes

5 garlic cloves, sliced

2 red onions, halved and thinly sliced

1 celery stalk, finely chopped

250 ml (9 fl oz/1 cup) red wine

1 teaspoon fresh thyme, chopped

300 g (10½ oz) button mushrooms

½ cup flat-leaf (Italian) parsley, roughly chopped

1 x 375 g (13 oz) block puff pastry

1 egg yolk, lightly beaten

to serve

spicy tomato relish (store-bought, or see page 47)

Preheat the oven to 180°C (350°F/Gas 4). Place the flour and paprika in a bowl and stir to combine. Season with the salt and pepper. Add the beef and toss until covered in flour. Place in an ovenproof casserole dish. Add the tomatoes, garlic, onion, celery, red wine and thyme and stir. Cover and cook for 1½ hours, stirring occasionally. Add the mushrooms, cover and return to the oven. Cook, stirring occasionally, for 1 hour, or until the sauce is thickened slightly and the beef and mushrooms are tender. Remove from the oven and stir through the parsley. The filling can be made up to a day in advance to this stage. Increase the oven temperature to 200°C (400°F/Gas 6).

On a lightly floured surface, roll out the pastry until 3 mm (⅛ inch) thick. Using the top of a 375 ml (13 fl oz/1½ cup) ovenproof ramekin (dariole mould) as a template, cut out six circles of pastry, leaving 1 cm (½ inch) extra around the circumference.

Divide the pie filling into six 375 ml (13 fl oz/1½ cup) ovenproof ramekins and cover with pastry, pushing down the edges around the rim. Make a cut in the pastry top with a sharp knife to allow any steam to escape and brush with the egg yolk. Bake for 20–25 minutes or until the pastry is lightly golden and the filling is hot. Serve with spicy tomato relish.

rice noodles with prawns and lime

SERVES 2

125 g (4½ oz) dried rice noodles

10 raw prawns (shrimp), peeled, deveined and halved lengthways

2 tablespoons korma curry paste

2 tablespoons light-flavoured oil (I like canola)

2 eggs, lightly beaten

4 spring onions (scallions), cut into 5 cm (2 inch) lengths

125 ml (4 fl oz/½ cup) chicken stock

2 tablespoons soy sauce

to serve

fresh coriander (cilantro) sprigs

lime wedges

Put the noodles in a bowl and soak in hot water for about 5 minutes or until soft. Drain well and set aside. Put the prawns in a bowl with the curry paste and stir until the prawns are well coated.

Heat a large frying pan or wok over a high heat. Add 1 tablespoon of the oil and pour in the eggs. Leave to set for 10 seconds, then push the eggs to the centre of the pan, almost scrambling them. When the eggs are about three-quarters cooked, remove them from the pan.

Wipe out the pan or wok with paper towels and return to the heat. Add the remaining oil and the prawns and stir gently for 1–2 minutes, then add the spring onions and stir-fry for 1 minute. Add the stock, soy sauce and noodles and stir-fry for 1–2 minutes until heated through. Add the egg, toss to combine and remove from the heat. Divide between two bowls and serve with coriander sprigs and lime wedges.

This is a dish that's very adaptable to whatever happens to be in your fridge. Chicken instead of prawns is an easy variation.

219

baked meatballs with tomatoes

SERVES 4–6

500 g (1 lb 2 oz) minced (ground) beef
or pork and veal
1 small onion, grated
55 g (2 oz/⅔ cup) fresh white breadcrumbs
3 tablespoons fresh flat-leaf (Italian)
parsley, chopped
3 tablespoons fresh coriander (cilantro)
leaves, chopped
1 egg, lightly beaten
1 teaspoon ground cumin
1 teaspoon sweet paprika
2 large fresh red chillies, finely chopped
sea salt
freshly ground black pepper
3 tablespoons olive oil
2 x 400 g (14 oz) tins chopped tomatoes
½ teaspoon sugar

to serve
roast chilli potatoes (see below)

Preheat the oven to 220°C (425°F/Gas 7). Combine the mince, onion, breadcrumbs, parsley, coriander, egg, cumin, paprika, half of the chilli and plenty of salt and pepper in a large bowl. Mix gently with your hands, then shape into small balls (I find wetting my hands makes this easier).

Toss the meatballs gently in the oil in a roasting tin and bake for 10–15 minutes. Transfer them to a frying pan over a medium heat and add the tomatoes, sugar, remaining chilli and some more salt and pepper. Stir the meatballs carefully to coat and then simmer for 20 minutes. Serve with the roast chilli potatoes.

1 kg (2 lb 4 oz) potatoes, peeled and
roughly diced
2 tablespoons olive oil
sea salt
1 large fresh red chilli, thinly sliced
3 spring onions (scallions), thinly sliced
small handful of fresh coriander (cilantro)
leaves, chopped

ROAST CHILLI POTATOES
Preheat the oven to 220°C (425°F/Gas 7). Toss the potatoes with the olive oil, place on a large baking tray and season with sea salt. Roast for 40 minutes, turning once, until golden and crispy. Scatter with the chilli, spring onions and coriander leaves and return to the oven for another 2 minutes before serving.

bistecca alla pizzaiola

SERVES 2

2 T-bone steaks, 2 cm (¾ inch) thick

extra virgin olive oil, for brushing

sea salt

freshly ground black pepper

125 ml (4 fl oz/½ cup) white wine

250 ml (9 fl oz/1 cup) good-quality tomato pasta sauce

¼ teaspoon dried chilli flakes

1 tablespoon fresh oregano

to serve

1 tablespoon fresh flat-leaf (Italian) parsley, chopped

crispy potatoes (see below)

Heat a large frying pan over high heat. Brush both sides of the steaks with olive oil and season well with salt and pepper. Cook the steaks for 1 minute on each side until brown, then remove from the pan and set aside. Add the wine to the hot pan and stir for 1 minute to reduce slightly. Stir in the pasta sauce, chilli and oregano.

Put the steaks back in the pan, reduce the heat to medium and cook for 5 minutes, turning once. Sprinkle with parsley and serve with crispy potatoes.

CRISPY POTATOES

6 small new potatoes

sea salt

3 tablespoons grated parmesan cheese

2 tablespoons olive oil

freshly ground black pepper

1 teaspoon lemon zest

1 garlic clove, crushed

Preheat the oven to 220°C (425°F/Gas 7). Boil the potatoes in salted water for about 15 minutes until tender. Drain and leave to cool slightly.

Put the potatoes on a baking tray and flatten slightly with the palm of your hand (or a fork or potato masher). Mix together the parmesan, olive oil, salt, pepper, lemon zest and garlic and sprinkle over the potatoes. Bake for 25 minutes until crispy.

giovanni's sausages with potatoes and rosemary

SERVES 4

6 Italian-style sausages

800 g (1 lb 12 oz) potatoes, scrubbed and sliced (I use kipfler/fingerling)

1½ teaspoons paprika

2 rosemary stalks

sea salt

freshly ground black pepper

½ loaf ciabatta, crust removed

50 ml (1¾ fl oz) extra virgin olive oil

to serve

handful fresh basil leaves

rocket (arugula) leaves

Preheat the oven to 200°C (400°F/Gas 6). Slice the sausages thickly and place in a large roasting tin. Add the potatoes, paprika, rosemary, salt and pepper. Tear the ciabatta into bite-sized pieces and add to the tin. Drizzle with the oil and toss gently.

Roast, stirring occasionally, for 30–40 minutes or until the potatoes are tender and the sausages and bread are golden brown. Sprinkle with the basil and serve with a salad of rocket leaves.

stir-fried noodles with beef and sugar snaps

SERVES 4 ADULTS OR LOTS OF CHILDREN

3 tablespoons oyster sauce
2 tablespoons soy sauce
1½ tablespoons dry sherry
3 tablespoons chicken stock
2 teaspoons sugar
1 tablespoon light-flavoured oil
(I like canola)
400 g (14 oz) beef fillet or rump, sliced
4 cm (1½ inch) piece of fresh ginger,
julienned or grated
200 g (7 oz) sugar snap peas

to serve
250 g (9 oz) fresh egg noodles

Bring a large pot of salted water to a rapid boil. Cook the noodles for 1–2 minutes or until tender, drain.

Stir together the oyster sauce, soy sauce, sherry, stock and sugar in a small bowl.

Heat a wok or large frying pan over high heat. Add the oil and, when it is smoking, stir-fry the beef in two batches, cooking for 1 minute until it is sealed and browned. Remove from the wok and set aside. Stir-fry the ginger and peas for 2 minutes, adding a little more oil if needed. Add the beef and sauce and cook for 1 minute, until the sauce has thickened slightly.

Divide the noodles among four bowls and top with the stir-fry. (Or add the noodles to the wok and mix it all together.)

crispy-skinned salmon with anchovy vinaigrette, fennel and green beans

SERVES 4

4 x 180 g (6¼ oz) salmon fillets, skin on
2 tablespoons olive oil
sea salt
freshly ground black pepper
2 baby fennel bulbs, finely sliced
250 g (9 oz) baby green beans, trimmed
and blanched
small handful of fresh flat-leaf (Italian)
parsley

to serve
anchovy vinaigrette (see below)

I small garlic clove
4 anchovies
100 ml (3½ fl oz) extra virgin olive oil
50 ml (1¾ fl oz) red wine vinegar
freshly ground black pepper

Heat a frying pan over a medium–high heat for 2 minutes. Brush the salmon with oil and season well with salt and pepper. Cook the salmon, skin side down, for 3 minutes, then turn over and cook for another minute. Remove from the pan and leave to rest for 2 minutes. The salmon should be quite rare and the skin crispy.

Arrange the fennel, beans and parsley on plates. Place the salmon on top and drizzle with anchovy vinaigrette to serve.

ANCHOVY VINAIGRETTE

In a mortar and pestle, pound the garlic and anchovies to a rough paste. Add the olive oil and red wine vinegar and stir together. Season with pepper (you probably won't need salt).

ocean trout with red chilli and tomatoes

SERVES 4

1 tablespoon olive oil, plus a little extra

4 x 200 g (7 oz) ocean trout fillets, skin on

2 large fresh red chillies, sliced

5 cm (2 inch) piece of fresh ginger, grated

3 garlic cloves, sliced

400 g (14 oz) tomatoes, chopped

2 tablespoons soy sauce

1½ tablespoons sugar

to serve

steamed rice

baby English spinach leaves

Heat the oil in a large frying pan over a medium–high heat. Add the trout and cook for 2 minutes on each side or until cooked to your taste. Remove from the pan.

Reduce the heat to medium and add a little extra oil. Add the chilli, ginger and garlic and cook for 2 minutes until golden. Add the tomatoes, soy sauce and sugar and cook for 5 minutes, stirring occasionally until thickened.

Serve the trout with steamed rice, baby English spinach leaves and the sauce spooned over the top.

stir-fried ginger fish with broccolini

SERVES 2

1 tablespoon light-flavoured oil
(I like canola)
4 tablespoons fresh ginger, julienned
350 g (12 oz) firm white fish fillets, skin on
(I like blue-eye trevalla or snapper),
cut into bite-sized pieces
8 spring onions (scallions), cut into
long lengths
200 g (7 oz) broccolini, sliced on the
diagonal and blanched
2 tablespoons fish sauce
2 teaspoons sugar
1 teaspoon sea salt
2 tablespoons lime juice

to serve
steamed jasmine rice

Heat a wok over a medium–high heat. Add the oil and, when hot, stir-fry the ginger for 1 minute. Add the fish and stir-fry for 3 minutes. Add the spring onions, broccolini, fish sauce, sugar and salt and gently stir-fry for another minute. Remove from the heat, add the lime juice and serve with steamed jasmine rice.

To julienne ginger, choose a large piece of fresh ginger and trim to make a rectangle. Slice thinly and then cut the slices into matchsticks.

sticky spare ribs

SERVES 6

2 pork spare rib racks (around
1.3 kg/3 lb each)

sea salt

freshly ground black pepper

4 garlic cloves, crushed

2 tablespoons finely grated fresh ginger

250 ml (9 fl oz/1 cup) soy sauce

125 ml (4 fl oz/½ cup) honey

3 tablespoons shaoxing rice wine, or dry
sherry

1 teaspoon five-spice

125 ml (4 fl oz/½ cup) hoisin sauce

to serve

snow peas (mangetout), steamed

steamed rice

Preheat the oven to 160°C (315°F/Gas 2–3). Put the ribs on a baking tray and season generously with salt and pepper. Roast for 1 hour.

Meanwhile, put the garlic, ginger, soy sauce, honey, shaoxing rice wine, five-spice and hoisin sauce in a small saucepan over a medium heat and cook for 15 minutes, stirring occasionally, until thick.

Baste the ribs with the sauce and cook for another 20 minutes. Put the ribs on a chopping board, brush again with the sauce and cut into individual ribs to serve.

butterflied lamb with romesco sauce

SERVES 6

1.8 kg (4 lb) butterflied lamb leg, cut into
two pieces
3 tablespoons olive oil
sea salt
freshly ground black pepper

to serve
romesco sauce (see below)
virgin paella (see below)
lemon wedges
small handful of fresh flat-leaf (Italian)
parsley

Preheat the oven to 180°C (350°F/Gas 4). Heat an ovenproof frying pan over high heat. Rub the lamb with the oil and season well with salt and pepper. Put the lamb skin side down in the pan and sear for 5 minutes, then turn over and cook for 2 minutes. Put the pan in the oven and roast for 15 minutes. Cover loosely with foil and rest for 10 minutes. Slice thickly and serve with romesco sauce, lemon wedges and parsley.

ROMESCO SAUCE

4 red capsicums (peppers), roasted,
peeled and seeded
4 tablespoons blanched almonds, toasted
1 tablespoon red wine vinegar
2 tablespoons extra virgin olive oil
sea salt
freshly ground black pepper

Put all the ingredients in a blender and pulse until the sauce is combined but still has some texture.

VIRGIN PAELLA

1 tablespoon olive oil
1 white onion, chopped
425 g (15 oz/2 cups) paella rice
125 ml (4 fl oz/½ cup) white wine
1.25 litres (44 fl oz/5 cups) chicken stock
6 saffron threads
sea salt

Heat the oil in a large, heavy-based deep frying pan or paella pan over a low–medium heat and cook the onion for 5 minutes until soft and golden. Add the rice and cook for 1 minute, stirring to coat. Add the wine and cook for 1 minute. Add the stock and saffron and cook, stirring occasionally, for 15 minutes or until the rice is just cooked. Season with salt and serve.

braised chicken with lemon and honey

SERVES 4

1 tablespoon olive oil

1.6 kg (3 lb 8 oz) chicken, cut into 8 pieces

1 red onion, sliced

12 garlic cloves, peeled but left whole

1 lemon, cut into chunks

185 ml (6 fl oz/¾ cup) chicken stock

125 ml (4 fl oz/½ cup) honey

small handful of fresh oregano

to serve

shepherd's salad with feta (see below)

Heat a large frying pan over a high heat, add the oil and chicken and cook for 5 minutes until golden. Remove and set aside. Reduce the heat to medium–high, add the onion and cook for 1 minute. Add the garlic and cook for 1 minute.

Return the chicken to the pan with the lemon, chicken stock and honey, reduce the heat, cover the pan and simmer for 20 minutes or until the chicken is cooked through. Lift out the chicken and put on a baking tray. Increase the heat under the sauce, and simmer, uncovered, for another 15 minutes to thicken. Place the chicken under a hot grill (broiler) until crisp. Arrange the chicken on a platter, drizzle with the sauce and sprinkle with oregano. Serve with shepherd's salad with feta.

SHEPHERD'S SALAD WITH FETA

400 g (14 oz) tin chickpeas, rinsed

150 g (5½ oz) feta cheese, crumbled

small handful of fresh lat-leaf (Italian) parsley

2 Lebanese (short) cucumbers, chopped

1 green capsicum (pepper), chopped

50 g (1¾ oz/⅓ cup) black olives, pitted and halved

dressing

3 tablespoons olive oil

1 tablespoon lemon juice

sea salt

freshly ground black pepper

Gently mix together the chickpeas, feta, parsley, cucumber, capsicum and olives in a large bowl. To make the dressing, whisk the olive oil and lemon juice and season with salt and pepper. Toss the dressing with the salad.

herbed chicken schnitzel

4 chicken breasts, skin removed

60 g (2¼ oz/½ cup) plain (all-purpose) flour

freshly ground black pepper

1 teaspoon sea salt

1 egg

2 tablespoons milk

160 g (5¾ oz/2 cups) fresh breadcrumbs

3 tablespoons fresh flat-leaf (Italian) parsley, chopped

3 tablespoons fresh chervil, chopped

3 tablespoons fresh oregano, chopped

1 tablespoon butter

125 ml (4 fl oz/½ cup) olive oil

to serve

mashed potatoes

Put each chicken breast between two sheets of plastic wrap and flatten slightly with a meat mallet or rolling pin. Cut each flattened breast in half. Put the flour in a shallow bowl and season with pepper and the salt. In a second bowl, lightly beat the egg and milk together. Mix the breadcrumbs and fresh herbs in a third bowl and season with salt and pepper. Dip each chicken fillet in flour to coat, then in the egg mixture and lastly in the breadcrumbs.

Heat the butter and olive oil in a large non-stick frying pan over a medium heat and cook the schnitzels for 3 minutes on each side until golden brown and cooked through (don't overcrowd the pan: cook them in batches if necessary). Drain on paper towels and keep warm until all the chicken is cooked.

FENNEL 'SLAW

3 fennel bulbs, thinly sliced

2 tablespoons small salted capers, rinsed

1 small red onion, thinly sliced

1½ tablespoons fresh flat-leaf (Italian) parsley, chopped

3 tablespoons whole-egg mayonnaise

1½ tablespoons lemon juice

sea salt

freshly ground black pepper

Put the fennel, capers, onion and parsley in a bowl. Mix together the mayonnaise and lemon juice and stir through the 'slaw. Season with sea salt and black pepper to serve.

broccolini and tofu sambal

2 tablespoons peanut oil
375 g (13 oz) firm tofu, cut into strips
1 onion, cut into thin wedges
½ teaspoon sea salt
2 garlic cloves, finely chopped
2 bunches broccolini, cut into long florets
2 teaspoons sambal oelek (optional)
2 tablespoons light soy sauce
1 tablespoon lemon juice

to serve
steamed rice

Heat half the oil in a wok or frying pan over a high heat. Cook the tofu in batches for 2 minutes on each side until it is golden brown. Lift out of the wok and set aside.

Return the wok to high heat and add the remaining oil, onion and salt. Stir-fry for 1 minute, then add the garlic and broccolini and cook for another 2 minutes. Add the sambal oelek, if using, and soy sauce and toss through. Add the tofu and stir in the lemon juice. Serve immediately with steamed rice.

moroccan fish stew

SERVES 4

1 tablespoon olive oil
1 large onion, thinly sliced
1 garlic clove, crushed
2 teaspoons grated fresh ginger
1 teaspoon ground cumin
1 teaspoon turmeric
1 cinnamon stick
pinch of cayenne pepper
400 g (14 oz) tin chopped tomatoes
sea salt
500 g (1 lb 2 oz) firm white fish fillets. such as blue-eye trevalla, snapper or ling, cut into chunks
400 g (14 oz) tin chickpeas, rinsed
2 teaspoons honey
freshly ground black pepper

to serve
fresh coriander (cilantro) leaves
flaked almonds, lightly toasted

Heat the olive oil in a large heavy-based frying pan over a medium–low heat. Add the onion and cook, stirring occasionally, for 5 minutes, or until the onion is translucent. Add the garlic, ginger, cumin, turmeric and cinnamon and cook, stirring, for 2 minutes, or until fragrant.

Add the cayenne, tomatoes, a pinch of sea salt and 250 ml (9 fl oz/1 cup) of water and cook, stirring frequently, for 10 minutes. Add the fish and simmer for 5 minutes, or until the fish is just tender. Add the chickpeas and honey and cook for a further 2–3 minutes. Season to taste with salt and pepper. Serve garnished with coriander and flaked almonds.

lime, paprika and honey glazed chicken

SERVES 4

2 tablespoons plain (all-purpose) flour

2 teaspoons paprika

sea salt

freshly ground black pepper

8 chicken legs

2 red onions, cut into wedges

2 tablespoons olive oil

2 tablespoons grated fresh ginger

1 garlic clove, crushed

2 tablespoons honey

125 ml (4 fl oz/½ cup) chicken stock

1 lime, cut into thin wedges

to serve

steamed rice

Asian greens

fresh coriander (cilantro) leaves

Preheat the oven to 220°C (425°F/Gas 7). Mix the flour and paprika and season with salt and pepper. Dust the chicken legs in the flour and then put in a large roasting tin with the onions. Drizzle with the olive oil and roast for 20 minutes, turning the chicken once during this time.

Mix together the ginger, garlic, honey and chicken stock. Pour over the chicken and add the lime wedges to the tin. Roast for another 10 minutes, or until the chicken is golden and glazed.

Serve with steamed rice, Asian greens and lots of coriander leaves.

spaghetti with garlic and spinach

SERVES 4

400 g (14 oz) spaghetti

80 ml (2½ fl oz/⅓ cup) extra virgin olive oil

6 garlic cloves, thinly sliced

sliced fresh red chilli, to taste (I like to use 2 small ones)

80 ml (2½ fl oz/⅓ cup) white wine

90 g (3¼ oz/2 cups) baby English spinach

to serve

sea salt

freshly ground black pepper

freshly grated parmesan cheese

Cook the spaghetti in a large pot of rapidly boiling salted water until *al dente* and drain. Meanwhile, put the olive oil, garlic and chilli in a frying pan over a medium heat and cook, stirring often, for about 5 minutes until the garlic is golden. Add the wine and cook, stirring, for 20 seconds. Add the drained pasta and spinach and toss to coat it well. Season with salt and pepper, then serve with lots of grated parmesan cheese.

sausages with caramelised onions and parmesan mash

4 red onions, quartered (or cut into
eighths, if large)
2 tablespoons soft brown sugar
½ teaspoon chilli flakes
sea salt
freshly ground black pepper
2 tablespoons extra virgin olive oil
2 tablespoons red wine vinegar or
balsamic vinegar
8 good-quality sausages

to serve
parmesan mash (see below)

Preheat the oven to 200°C (400°F/Gas 6). Put the onions in a
baking dish and sprinkle with the sugar, chilli flakes, salt and pepper.
Drizzle with olive oil and vinegar and bake for 35 minutes.

Cook the sausages in a frying pan over a medium–high heat for
about 15 minutes until well browned. Serve with the caramelised
onions and parmesan mash.

PARMESAN MASH

800 g (1 lb 12 oz) desiree potatoes, peeled
and cut into chunks
125 ml (4 fl oz/½ cup) milk
25 g (1 oz) butter
35 g (1¼ oz/⅓ cup) finely grated
parmesan cheese
sea salt
freshly ground black pepper

Cook the potatoes in boiling salted water until tender, then drain
and mash. Heat the milk and butter in a saucepan until the butter
has melted and then beat into the mash until smooth. Add the
parmesan and beat well. Season with salt and pepper.

beef and noodle stir-fry with asian greens

375 g (13 oz) fresh rice noodles

2 teaspoons sesame oil

3 tablespoons oyster sauce

2 tablespoons dark soy sauce

1½ tablespoons dry sherry or shaoxing rice wine

3 tablespoons chicken stock

2 teaspoons sugar

1 tablespoon peanut oil

600 g (1 lb 5 oz) beef fillet or rump, thinly sliced

4 cm (1½ inch) piece of fresh ginger, julienned or grated

1 bunch Chinese broccoli (gai larn), stalks removed and halved, leaves halved

Cover the noodles in boiling salted water according to the packet instructions. Drain and toss with the sesame oil. Meanwhile, stir together the oyster sauce, soy sauce, sherry, stock and sugar.

Heat a wok or large frying pan over a high heat. Add the peanut oil and, when smoking, add the beef in two batches, cooking for 1 minute to seal and brown. Remove and set aside. Add the ginger and Chinese broccoli, adding a little extra oil if needed, and stir-fry for 2 minutes. Add the beef and sauce and cook for another minute to slightly reduce the sauce.

Either toss the noodles through the sauce in the wok, or spoon them into bowls and top with the beef stir-fry.

spicy chicken meatballs

3 tablespoons olive oil

1 small onion, finely diced

2 garlic cloves, crushed

½ teaspoon ground coriander

1 large fresh red chilli, thinly sliced

500 g (1 lb 2 oz) minced (ground) chicken

3 tablespoons fresh breadcrumbs

50 g (1¾ oz) pancetta, chopped

2 tablespoons fresh flat-leaf (Italian)
parsley, chopped

sea salt

500 g (1 lb 2 oz) cherry tomatoes, halved

freshly ground black pepper

125 ml (4 fl oz/½ cup) chicken stock

to serve

500 g (1 lb 2 oz) wholemeal (whole-wheat)
fusilli, cooked

parmesan cheese shavings

Preheat the oven to 200°C (400°F/Gas 6). Heat 1 tablespoon of the olive oil in a saucepan over a medium-high heat. Add the onion and garlic and cook, stirring, for 5 minutes, or until the onion is soft. Add the coriander and chilli and cook for 1 minute. Set aside to cool completely.

Put the chicken in a bowl with the breadcrumbs, pancetta, parsley and salt. Add the spiced onion and mix well with your hands. Refrigerate for 30 minutes to firm the mixture. Wet your hands with cold water to stop the mixture sticking and roll it into small meatballs.

Put the cherry tomatoes on a baking tray lined with baking paper, drizzle with 1 tablespoon of the olive oil and season with salt and pepper. Put the meatballs on a second lined tray and drizzle with the remaining oil. Roast the tomatoes and meatballs in the oven for 15–20 minutes, or until the meatballs are golden and the tomatoes are starting to pucker.

Put the stock and tomatoes in a saucepan and add the meatballs. Simmer for 5 minutes and season to taste before spooning over pasta and serving with parmesan shavings.

oven-baked chicken and asparagus risotto

SERVES 4

2 tablespoons olive oil

500 g (1 lb 2 oz) boneless chicken breasts, cut into thin strips

1 onion, finely chopped

1 garlic clove, crushed

1 teaspoon finely grated lemon zest

250 g (9 oz) arborio rice

750 ml (26 fl oz/3 cups) chicken stock

175 g (6 oz/1 bunch) asparagus, sliced on the diagonal

35 g (1¼ oz/⅓ cup) grated parmesan cheese, plus extra to serve

sea salt

freshly ground black pepper

Preheat the oven to 180°C (350°F/Gas 4). Heat 1 tablespoon of the olive oil in a large flameproof casserole dish over a high heat. Add the chicken and cook, stirring frequently, for 3–4 minutes, or until golden brown. Remove and set aside.

Add the remaining olive oil and the onion to the casserole and cook, stirring occasionally, for 5 minutes, or until the onion is soft. Add the garlic and lemon zest and cook, stirring, for 30 seconds. Add the rice and stir to coat in the oil. Add the stock and bring to the boil, stirring occasionally.

Cover the casserole and put in the oven for 15 minutes. Add the asparagus, return the chicken to the casserole and bake for a further 3–4 minutes, or until the asparagus is bright green and just tender. Stir in the parmesan and season with salt and pepper, before serving with extra parmesan.

lamb biryani

SERVES 4 TO 6

1 kg (2 lb 4 oz) boneless lamb leg, trimmed and diced

1 tablespoon garam masala

2 teaspoons ground cumin

½ teaspoon turmeric

2 tablespoons olive oil

1 onion, thinly sliced

2 garlic cloves, crushed

2 teaspoons finely grated fresh ginger

300 g (10½ oz/1½ cups) basmati rice

750 ml (26 fl oz/3 cups) chicken stock

small handful of fresh coriander (cilantro) leaves

to serve

cumin, mint and coriander yoghurt (see below)

Preheat the oven to 200°C (400°F/Gas 6). Put the lamb in a large bowl with the garam masala, cumin and turmeric and toss to coat the lamb in the spices. Heat 1 tablespoon of the oil in a flameproof casserole over a medium heat, add the lamb in batches and cook, stirring occasionally, for 3–4 minutes until browned all over, adding a little more oil if necessary. Remove and set aside.

Add the remaining oil, onion, garlic and ginger to the casserole dish and cook over a medium heat until the onion is soft and pale golden. Add the rice, stir together and cook for 2 minutes. Return the lamb to the casserole in a single layer and carefully pour in the stock. Put the lid on the casserole and put in the oven. Cook for 35–45 minutes, or until the rice is tender and has absorbed all the liquid. Top with coriander leaves and serve with cumin, mint and coriander yoghurt

CUMIN, MINT AND CORIANDER YOGHURT

300 g (10 oz) natural yoghurt

1 teaspoon ground cumin

2 tablespoons finely fresh mint, chopped

2 tablespoons fresh coriander (cilantro) leaves, finely chopped

2 cm (¾ inch) piece of fresh ginger, grated

large fresh green chilli, seeded and finely chopped

sea salt

freshly ground black pepper

lightly toasted cumin seeds

Stir together the yoghurt, cumin, mint, coriander, ginger and chilli. Season well with salt and pepper and sprinkle with cumin seeds. Serve as an accompaniment to curries.

259

fragrant chicken and spinach curry

SERVES 4

2 tablespoons vegetable oil

1 large onion, chopped

2 teaspoons ground coriander

½ teaspoon turmeric

pinch of cayenne pepper

2 garlic cloves, crushed

1 tablespoon grated fresh ginger

750 g (1 lb 10 oz) boneless chicken thighs, cubed

400 g (14 oz) tin chopped tomatoes

½ teaspoon sea salt

2 teaspoons soft brown sugar

1 tablespoon lime juice

90 g (3¼ oz/2 cups) baby English spinach, finely chopped

large handful of fresh coriander (cilantro) leaves, chopped

to serve

steamed rice

Heat the oil in a large heavy-based frying pan over a medium heat. Add the onion and cook, stirring, for 5–6 minutes until the onion is soft. Add the spices, garlic and ginger and cook, stirring, for 2 more minutes. Add the chicken and increase the heat to medium-high. Cook, stirring often, for 5 minutes, or until the chicken is browned.

Stir in the tomatoes and salt and bring to simmering point. Reduce the heat to low, cover the pan and simmer gently for 15 minutes. Add the sugar, lime juice and spinach and stir until the spinach has just wilted. Remove from the heat, sprinkle with coriander and serve with steamed rice.

ricotta- and herb-stuffed roast chicken

SERVES 4

1.6 kg (3 lb 8 oz) free-range chicken

375 g (13 oz/1½ cups) fresh ricotta cheese

2 tablespoons fresh chives, snipped

2 tablespoons fresh chervil, chopped

2 teaspoons finely grated lemon zest

sea salt

freshly ground black pepper

olive oil

Preheat the oven to 200°C (400°F/Gas 6). To spatchcock the chicken, place the bird, breast side down, on a chopping board. Using poultry shears or a sharp knife, cut along both sides of the backbone, cutting through the skin and bone. Remove the backbone. Turn the bird over and press firmly on the breast bone to break the bone and flatten the breast. Tuck the wing tips under the breast.

Mix together the ricotta, herbs, lemon zest, salt and pepper. With your fingers, carefully loosen the skin over the breast of the chicken and down to the thigh area. Spread the ricotta mixture evenly under the skin to cover the breast and thigh.

Put the chicken in a roasting tin, drizzle with olive oil and season with salt and pepper. Roast for 50 minutes, or until the juices run clear when you insert a skewer into the thickest part of the thigh. Leave to rest for 5 minutes before carving.

SERVES 4 # light laksa

1 teaspoon peanut oil

1 tablespoon red curry paste

1 litre (35 fl oz/4 cups) chicken stock

150 ml (5 fl oz) coconut milk

2 makrut (kaffir lime) leaves, plus extra leaves, thinly sliced, to garnish

3 cm (1¼ inch) piece of fresh ginger, sliced

500 g (1 lb 2 oz) boneless chicken breasts

150 g (5½ oz) rice vermicelli

soft brown sugar and lime juice, to taste

1 bunch baby bok choy (pak choy), leaves separated

90 g (3¼ oz/1 cup) trimmed bean sprouts

Heat the oil in a large saucepan over a medium heat. Add the curry paste and cook, stirring, for 1–2 minutes, or until fragrant. Add the stock, coconut milk, makrut leaves and ginger.

Increase the heat to high and bring to the boil. Then reduce the heat to very low, add the chicken, cover the pan and poach the chicken gently for 7 minutes, or until just cooked through. Remove the chicken and set aside to cool slightly, then shred.

Put the rice vermicelli in a bowl and pour in enough boiling water to cover. Soak for 6–7 minutes, then drain.

Season the soup with the brown sugar and lime juice, to taste. Divide the rice vermicelli, shredded chicken, bok choy and bean sprouts among four large bowls. Pour in the hot soup and garnish with thinly sliced makrut leaves.

white bean and chorizo soup

1 teaspoon olive oil

1 chorizo sausage (about 150 g/5½ oz), diced

1 large onion, thinly sliced

2 celery stalks, diced

2 garlic cloves, crushed

2 teaspoons fresh thyme , chopped

1 teaspoon paprika

2 tomatoes, diced

1 litre (35 fl oz/4 cups) chicken stock

2 x 400 g (14 oz) tins cannellini beans, rinsed

sea salt

freshly ground black pepper

Heat the olive oil in a large sauce pan over a high heat and cook the chorizo for 3–4 minutes until crisp. Drain on paper towels.

Reduce the heat to medium-low, add the onion and celery to the pan and cook, stirring occasionally, for 6–7 minutes until softened. Add the garlic, thyme and paprika and cook, stirring, for 1–2 minutes until fragrant. Add the tomatoes and cook for another minute.

Return the chorizo to the pan with the stock and bring to the boil, then reduce the heat and simmer, stirring occasionally, for 10 minutes. Add the beans and cook for another 5 minutes. Season with salt and pepper before serving.

dessert

Desserts are one of the real pleasures that have been sacrificed in an effort to cram more into a day. To me, dessert is something to linger over. It provides the ideal moment for savouring the day and incites some of the best compliments!

Sweet things have a bad reputation but I'm a great fan of moderation and there's nothing wrong with the occasional bit of butter and sugar. As a cook, nothing gives me more satisfaction than making sweet things for people to enjoy.

I adore pleasing people and dessert is a sure-fire way to anyone's heart.

honey cheesecake

60 g (2¼ oz/½ cup) sultanas (golden raisins)
60 ml (2 fl oz/¼ cup) Marsala, or cold weak tea
55 g (2 oz/¼ cup) caster (superfine) sugar
6 eggs
finely grated zest of 1 orange
90 g (3¼ oz/¼ cup) honey
1 kg (2 lb 4 oz) good-quality ricotta cheese, lightly mashed to break up any lumps
icing (confectioners') sugar, for dusting

to serve
125 g (4½ oz/1 cup) raspberries

Preheat the oven to 160°C (315°F/Gas 2–3). Place the sultanas and Marsala in a small bowl and leave to soak for 30 minutes.

Place the sugar and eggs in a large bowl and beat for 5 minutes, or until light and foamy. Drain the sultanas then fold through the egg mixture with the zest, honey and ricotta until combined.

Pour the batter into a 23 cm (9 inch) greased or non-stick springform cake tin. Bake for 1 hours, or until golden. The cake will wobble slightly in the centre.

Remove from the oven and leave to cool in the tin. Transfer the cake onto a serving platter, dust with icing sugar and serve with the raspberries.

Because this cake is so simple, I love to use fresh ricotta cheese cut from a wheel rather than from a tub. If you do find that your ricotta is watery, leave it to drain in a colander for 30 minutes before using.

yoghurt pannacotta with rose-scented plums

SERVES 8

375 ml (13 fl oz/1½ cups) cream
115 g (4 oz/½ cup) caster (superfine) sugar
1 vanilla bean, split lengthways
10 g (¼ oz) sachet of powdered gelatine
500 g (1 lb 2 oz/2 cups) skim milk yoghurt

to serve
rose-scented plums (see below)

Place the cream and sugar in a saucepan over a medium heat. Using the point of a knife, scrape the vanilla bean seeds into the saucepan before adding the entire bean. Stir until the sugar is dissolved, then just bring to the boil before removing from the heat. Discard the vanilla bean. Pour 125 ml (4 fl oz/½ cup) of the cream mixture into a small bowl, sprinkle the gelatine powder over the top and whisk with a fork until smooth. Pour back into the saucepan and stir until the gelatine has completely dissolved. (If you wish to use gelatine leaves instead, follow the manufacturer's instructions.) Add the yoghurt and whisk until smooth. Strain the mixture through a fine sieve and divide between eight 125 ml (4 fl oz/½ cup) moulds, cover with plastic wrap and chill for 3 hours, or until just set.

To serve, dip each mould into hot water for a few seconds, making sure the water only comes halfway up the sides. Place a plate on top and invert the pannacotta. Serve immediately with the rose-scented plums and a spoonful of plum syrup.

ROSE-SCENTED PLUMS

115 g (4 oz/½ cup) caster (superfine) sugar
1 tablespoon rosewater
8 ripe plums, sliced

Place the sugar and rosewater into a large deep frying pan with 500 ml (17 fl oz/2 cups) water.

Stir gently over a low heat until the sugar dissolves. Increase the heat to high and bring the syrup to the boil. Boil rapidly for 1 minute then add the plums. Allow the syrup to come back to the boil then reduce to a simmer. Cook, stirring occasionally, for 8–10 minutes, or until the fruit is tender. Remove the plums, increase the heat and boil the syrup for a few minutes or until reduced. Pour over the plums and allow to cool before serving.

chocolate self-saucing pudding

SERVES 4

125 g (4½ oz/1 cup) plain (all-purpose)
flour
a pinch of salt
15 g (4 oz/½ cup) caster (superfine) sugar
3 teaspoons baking powder
4 tablespoons cocoa powder
250 ml (9 fl oz/1 cup) milk
85 g (3 oz) unsalted butter, melted
2 eggs, lightly beaten
1 teaspoon natural vanilla extract

topping
185 g (6½ oz/1 cup) soft brown sugar
2 tablespoons cocoa powder
250 ml (9 fl oz/1 cup) boiling water

to serve
thick (double/heavy) cream

Preheat the oven to 180°C (350°F/Gas 4). Sift the flour, salt, sugar, baking powder and cocoa powder into a bowl. Add the milk, butter, egg and vanilla and mix with beaters until combined. Pour into four 250 ml (9 fl oz/1 cup) greased pudding moulds.

To make the topping, stir the brown sugar and cocoa powder in a bowl to combine, then sprinkle it over the pudding batter.

Pour 60 ml (2 fl oz/¼ **cup**) boiling water carefully and evenly over each pudding, then bake for 20–25 minutes. Serve with thick cream.

mandarin and almond cake

3 mandarins, unpeeled and scrubbed
230 g (8¼ oz/1 cup) caster (superfine) sugar
6 eggs
200 g (7 oz/2 cups) ground almonds

caramelised citrus zest
55 g (2 oz/¼ cup) caster (superfine) sugar
zest of 2 oranges
lightly whipped cream

Put the mandarins in a medium-sized saucepan and cover with water. Bring to the boil and simmer for 2 hours, adding water when necessary to keep the mandarins covered at all times.

Preheat the oven to 160°C (315°F/Gas 2–3). Drain the mandarins and cool to room temperature. Once cooled, split them open with your hands and remove any seeds.

Purée the mandarins, including the skins, in a food processor.

Whisk the sugar and eggs together in a large bowl until combined. Add the ground almonds and mandarin purée and stir thoroughly.

Pour the mixture into a well-greased 24 cm (9 inch) spring-form cake tin and bake for 1 hour 10 minutes, or until the cake looks set in the middle, springs back when touched and comes away from the edges. Remove from the oven and allow to cool in the tin.

To make the caramelised citrus zest, put the sugar in a saucepan with 60 ml (2 fl oz/¼ cup) of water over a low heat and stir until the sugar dissolves. Add the orange zest and boil the mixture until it just starts to caramelise. Lift the zest out with a fork and cool it on a plate. Serve the cake with lightly whipped cream and the caramelised citrus zest.

chocolate brownies with ice cream and warm chocolate sauce

SERVES 8

345 g (12 oz/1½ cups) caster (superfine) sugar
85 g (3 oz/⅔ cup) cocoa powder
60 g (2¼ oz/½ cup) plain (all-purpose) flour
1 teaspoon baking powder
4 eggs, beaten
200 g (7 oz) unsalted butter, melted
2 teaspoons natural vanilla extract
200 g (7 oz/1⅓ cups) dark chocolate buttons

to serve
good-quality vanilla ice cream
cocoa powder, for dusting (optional)
warm chocolate sauce (see below)

125 g (4½ oz) good-quality dark chocolate, chopped
185 ml (6 fl oz/¾ cup) cream

Preheat the oven to 160°C (315°F/Gas 2–3). Stir the sugar, cocoa powder, flour and baking powder together in a bowl. Add the eggs, melted butter and vanilla and mix until combined. Mix in the chocolate buttons. Pour into a lined 22 cm (9 inch) square tin and bake for 40–45 minutes.

Allow the brownie block to slightly cool then cut into eight pieces. Place on serving plates with a scoop of vanilla ice cream. Dust with cocoa powder if you like, then serve with the chocolate sauce.

WARM CHOCOLATE SAUCE
Put the chopped chocolate and the cream in a heatproof bowl and place the bowl over a saucepan of just simmering water. Whisk occasionally until a thick sauce forms. Cool slightly before serving.

apple and almond puddings

SERVES 6

150 g (5½ oz) unsalted butter
150 g (5½ oz) caster (superfine) sugar
3 granny smith apples, peeled, cored and sliced
1 teaspoon natural vanilla extract

batter
175 g (6 oz) unsalted butter, cubed
175 g (6 oz) caster (superfine) sugar
3 eggs
100 g (3½ oz/1 cup) ground almonds
100 g (3½ oz) plain (all-purpose) flour
2 teaspoons baking powder
1 teaspoon cinnamon

to serve
cream

Preheat the oven to 180°C (350°F/Gas 4). Place a saucepan over a medium to high heat and add the butter and sugar. Stir until the butter is melted and the sugar dissolved. Add the apple and vanilla and cook for 10 minutes, or until soft and caramelised.

To make the batter, cream the butter and sugar until pale and creamy. Add the eggs, one at a time, stirring until well combined. Fold in the ground almonds, flour, baking powder and cinnamon and mix until combined.

Lightly grease and line six 250 ml (9 fl oz/1 cup) ovenproof ramekins or dariole moulds. Arrange the caramelised apples on the bottom. Divide the batter evenly between the ramekins and smooth over with the back of a spoon. Cook for about 25 minutes, or until lightly golden.

Run a knife around the edge of each ramekin then invert onto a serving dish. Serve with cream.

chilled
zabaglione

SERVES 4

6 egg yolks
80 g (2¾ oz/⅓ cup) caster (superfine)
sugar
185 ml (6 fl oz/¾ cup) Marsala
finely grated zest of 1 lemon
½ teaspoon natural vanilla extract
185 ml (6 fl oz/¾ cup) cream, lightly
whipped

to serve
savoiardi (lady fingers) biscuits (optional)

Whisk the egg yolks, sugar, Marsala, lemon zest and vanilla in a heatproof bowl over a saucepan of simmering water for about 5–6 minutes, or until the mixture is light and frothy. Remove from the heat and allow to cool. Fold in the lightly whipped cream, then pour into four glasses or a serving dish. Chill for at least 2 hours.

Serve with savoiardi biscuits, if you wish.

It is really important to not leave the stove for this recipe — you don't want scrambled eggs!

284

blueberry trifle

55 g (2 oz/¼ cup) caster (superfine) sugar

1 tablespoon lemon juice

250 g (9 oz) blueberries

5 eggs, separated

115 g (4 oz/½ cup) caster (superfine) sugar, extra

1 vanilla bean, split lengthways, or 1 teaspoon natural vanilla extract

250 g (9 oz) mascarpone

½ pandoro, or 1 sponge cake, cut into 4 cm (1½ inch) slices

185 ml (6 fl oz/¾ cup) Marsala

45 g (1¾ oz/½ cup) flaked almonds, toasted

Place the sugar, lemon juice and 60 ml (2 fl oz/¼ cup) water in a small saucepan over a medium heat. Stir until the sugar is dissolved then bring to the boil. Add the blueberries, reduce the heat to low and simmer for 5 minutes. Leave to cool.

While the syrup is cooling, place the egg yolks and extra sugar in a bowl and beat until the mixture is pale and creamy. Using the point of a knife, scrape the vanilla bean seeds and add to the bowl. Add the mascarpone and beat until smooth.

Place the egg whites in a clean, dry stainless steel bowl and whisk until soft peaks form. Using a large metal spoon, fold lightly through the mascarpone mixture in two batches.

Line a 2 litre (70 fl oz/8 cup) serving bowl with a layer of pandoro or sponge cake, moisten with roughly a quarter of the Marsala, top with a quarter of the blueberries and syrup, and a quarter of the mascarpone mixture. Repeat the layering, reserving 2 tablespoons of the blueberries and syrup for garnishing, until you finish with a layer of the mascarpone mixture. Cover and refrigerate for 6 hours, or overnight, to allow the flavour to develop.

Remove the trifle from the refrigerator, drizzle over the reserved blueberries and syrup, and sprinkle with toasted flaked almonds.

little lemon puddings with yoghurt and blackberries

50 g (1¾ oz) unsalted butter

finely grated zest of 1 lemon

115 g (4 oz/½ cup) caster (superfine) sugar

2 eggs, separated

40 g (1½ oz/⅓ cup) plain (all-purpose) flour, sifted

300 ml (10½ fl oz/1¼ cups) milk

2 tablespoons lemon juice

to serve

plain yoghurt

250 g (9 oz) blackberries

icing (confectioners') sugar, for dusting

Preheat the oven to 180°C (350°F/Gas 4). Place the butter, zest and sugar in a bowl and beat until pale and creamy. Add the egg yolks, one at a time, beating well after each addition. Fold through the flour then gradually add the milk in a steady stream, whisking lightly to combine. Add the lemon juice and mix to combine. The mixture will look slightly curdled.

Place the egg whites in a clean, dry stainless steel bowl and whisk until stiff peaks form. Using a large metal spoon, fold lightly through the pudding batter. Pour the batter into four 250 ml (9 fl oz/1 cup) ovenproof ramekins or dariole moulds and place on a baking tray. Bake for 15 minutes, or until lightly browned. Place a dollop of yoghurt and the blackberries on top then dust with icing sugar.

apple and passionfruit crumble

SERVES 4

6 granny smith apples, peeled and
thinly sliced
110 g (3¾ oz/½ cup) sugar
pulp from 8 passionfruit

topping
100 g (3½ oz/1 cup) rolled (porridge) oats
125 g (4½ oz/⅔ cup) soft brown sugar
40 g (1½ oz/⅓ cup) plain (all-purpose)
flour
100 g (3½ oz) butter, softened

to serve
vanilla ice cream or thick (double/heavy)
cream

Preheat the oven to 180°C (350°F/Gas 4) and grease a 2 litre (70 fl oz/8 cup) baking dish. Mix together the apples, sugar and passionfruit pulp and put in the dish.

Using your fingertips, rub together the oats, brown sugar, flour and butter to make a crumbly topping. Sprinkle over the fruit and bake for 25–30 minutes until golden. Serve with ice cream or cream.

pistachio cake with orange blossom syrup

SERVES 10

140 g (5 oz/1 cup) pistachio nuts

6 eggs, separated

230 g (8¼ oz/1 cup) caster (superfine) sugar

185 g (6½ oz/¾ cup) plain yoghurt

125 ml (4 fl oz/½ cup) light-flavoured oil (I like light olive or canola)

150 g (5½ oz) plain (all-purpose) flour

1 teaspoon baking powder

a pinch of salt

to serve

orange blossom syrup (see below)

figs, halved

plain yoghurt

Preheat the oven to 180°C (350°F/Gas 4). Butter and flour a 26 cm (10½ inch) spring-form tin and line the base with baking paper. Finely grind the pistachios in a food processor. Beat the egg yolks and half the sugar until pale and very thick. Fold in the yoghurt and oil. Sift the flour, baking powder and salt over the mixture and fold through with the ground pistachios.

Beat the egg whites until soft peaks form. Gradually add the remaining sugar and beat until firm peaks form. Gently fold half into the cake mixture, then fold in the other half. Pour into the tin and bake for 30 minutes. Cover loosely with foil and bake for another 15 minutes, until a skewer inserted into the centre comes out clean. Leave to cool completely in the tin and then spoon orange blossom syrup over the top. Serve with fresh figs and yoghurt.

ORANGE BLOSSOM SYRUP

230 g (8¼ oz/1 cup) caster (superfine) sugar

125 ml (4 fl oz/½ cup) freshly squeezed orange juice

½ teaspoon orange blossom water

Put the sugar, orange juice and 125 ml (4 fl oz/½ cup) of water in a saucepan over a low heat and stir to dissolve. Increase the heat and boil for 10–12 minutes, or until syrupy. Remove from the heat and stir in the orange blossom water. Spoon over the cake while the syrup is still warm.

crema catalana

625 ml (21½ fl oz/2½ cups) cream
170 ml (5½ fl oz/⅔ cup) milk
2 teaspoons natural vanilla extract
2 cinnamon sticks
peel from 1 orange
peel from 1 lemon
6 egg yolks
4 tablespoons caster (superfine) sugar
2½ tablespoons soft brown sugar

Preheat the oven to 140°C (275°F/Gas 1). Put the cream, milk, vanilla, cinnamon, orange and lemon peel in a saucepan over a medium heat and bring just to boiling point, then remove from the heat.

Whisk together the egg yolks and caster sugar in a large bowl. Strain the cream and pour slowly over the yolk and sugar mixture, whisking constantly. Skim off any foam that rises to the top.

Put six 125 ml (4 fl oz/½ cup) ramekins or dariole moulds in a large roasting tin and spoon the mixture into the ramekins. Pour hot water into the tin to come halfway up the sides of the ramekins and cover the whole tin with foil. Bake for 30–35 minutes, or until just set. Lift the ramekins out of the roasting tin and leave to cool before chilling in the fridge for 2 hours.

Preheat the grill (broiler) to its hottest temperature. Put the ramekins on a baking tray, sprinkle brown sugar over the chilled creams and then place under the grill for a couple of minutes until the sugar is melted and dark golden (if you have a chef's blowtorch, this is the time to use it). Leave for a few minutes for the sugar to cool and harden before serving.

pavlova with yoghurt cream and strawberries

SERVES 8

6 egg whites
¼ teaspoon cream of tartar
1 teaspoon natural vanilla extract
310 g (11 oz/1⅓ cups) caster (superfine) sugar
1 tablespoon cornflour (cornstarch)
2 tablespoons arrowroot
2 teaspoons white vinegar

to serve
250 ml (9 fl oz/1 cup) cream, whipped
125 g (4 oz/½ cup) plain yoghurt
250 g (9 oz/1⅔ cup) strawberries, hulled and halved, if large
1 tablespoon icing (confectioners') sugar

Preheat the oven to 180°C (350°F/Gas 4) and line a baking tray with baking paper. Draw a circle on the paper about 20 cm (8 inches) in diameter.

Beat the egg whites, cream of tartar and vanilla in a clean, dry bowl until stiff peaks form. Add the sugar, a tablespoon at a time, beating continuously until the meringue is glossy and thick. Stir in the cornflour, arrowroot and vinegar.

Pile the meringue onto the circle on the baking tray and put in the oven. Immediately reduce the oven to 120°C (235°F/Gas ½) and bake the pavlova for 1 hour 20 minutes, or until the outside is firm but not browned. Turn off the oven and leave the pavlova inside, with the door ajar, until completely cooled.

Gently fold together the cream and yoghurt. Toss the strawberries with the icing sugar. Spoon the yoghurt cream over the pavlova and top with strawberries to serve.

white chocolate mousse with raspberry ripple

SERVES 6

250 g (9 oz) good-quality white chocolate, chopped
80 ml (2½ fl oz/⅓ cup) milk
1 teaspoon natural vanilla extract
3 eggs, separated
375 ml (13 fl oz/1½ cups) cream
250 g (9 oz/2 cups) raspberries

Place the white chocolate, milk and vanilla in a heatproof bowl over a saucepan of simmering water, making sure the bowl does not touch the water. Heat until the chocolate is just melted, stirring regularly. Allow to cool for 5 minutes. Add the egg yolks, beating well after each addition.

Whip the cream in a bowl until soft peaks form then fold through the chocolate mixture until just combined. Whisk the egg whites in a large, dry, clean stainless steel bowl until soft peaks form. Using a large metal spoon, fold through the chocolate mixture in two batches. Divide the mousse between six 250 ml (9 fl oz/1 cup) serving dishes. Using a fork, crush the raspberries in a separate bowl then swirl over the top of the mousse. Cover and chill for 3 to 4 hours, or until set.

This mousse is just as delicious with fresh passionfruit or crushed blackberries swirled in.

raspberry tarts

230 g (8 oz/1 cup) caster (superfine) sugar
300 g (10½ oz) fresh raspberries
250 g (9 oz/2 cups) plain (all-purpose) flour
125 g (4½ oz/1 cup) icing (confectioners')
sugar
a pinch of salt
180 g (6½ oz) unsalted butter, chilled
and cubed
60 ml (2 fl oz/¼ cup) iced water
165 g (5¾ oz/¾ cup) mascarpone
185 ml (6 fl oz/¾ cup) cream,
lightly whipped
1 teaspoon vanilla bean paste

To make a raspberry syrup, put the caster sugar in a pan with 60 ml (2 fl oz/¼ cup) of water and stir over a low heat to dissolve the sugar. Increase the heat and bring to the boil. Cook until golden, then remove from the heat. Mash 100 g (3½ oz) of the raspberries and stir into the syrup. Leave to cool.

Sift the flour, icing sugar and salt in a bowl and stir to combine. Using your fingertips, rub in the butter until the mixture resembles coarse breadcrumbs. Add the iced water and mix until the dough comes together in a ball. Wrap in plastic wrap and chill for 30 minutes. Roll out on a lightly floured surface until 3 mm (⅛ inch) thick, then press lightly into 12 individual tart tins and prick with a fork. Chill for a further 30 minutes.

Preheat the oven to 200°C (400°F/Gas 6). Line the chilled pastry with baking paper and add baking weights or uncooked rice. Bake for 10 minutes, then remove the paper and weights. Bake for another 10 minutes, or until the pastry is golden and crisp. Leave to cool.

Remove the pastry cases from the tins and arrange on a serving plate. Mix together the mascarpone, cream and vanilla bean paste and spoon into the tarts. Arrange the rest of the raspberries on top and drizzle with the raspberry syrup.

raspberry, pistachio and rosewater semifreddo

SERVES 6 TO 8

6 egg yolks
3 tablespoons honey
250 ml (9 fl oz/1 cup) cream, whipped
2 teaspoons rosewater
150 g (5½ oz) fresh raspberries, plus a few extra to serve
3 tablespoons pistachio nuts, chopped

Beat the egg yolks and honey together with electric beaters for 10 minutes, or until thick, pale, creamy and doubled in volume. Fold in the whipped cream and rosewater until just combined.

Line the base and two sides of a 1 litre (35 fl oz/4 cup) loaf (bar) tin with a piece of plastic wrap, leaving the wrap hanging over the sides of the tin. Spoon the mixture into the tin, fold the plastic over the top to cover the semifreddo and freeze for 1–2 hours, or until partially frozen. Remove from the freezer and stir through the raspberries and pistachios. Cover with plastic wrap and return to the freezer until completely frozen.

Before serving, leave to soften in the fridge for 20 minutes. Turn out of the tin, cut into slices and serve with a few extra raspberries.

sticky date cake with butterscotch sauce

SERVES 10

300 g (10½ oz/1⅔ cups) pitted dates, chopped

1 teaspoon bicarbonate of soda (baking soda)

70 g (2½ oz) unsalted butter, diced

170 g (6 oz/¾ cup) caster(superfine) sugar

1 teaspoon natural vanilla extract

2 eggs, lightly beaten

185 g (6½ oz/1½ cups) self-raising flour, sifted

to serve

butterscotch sauce (see below)

vanilla ice cream

Preheat the oven to 180°C (350°F/Gas 4). Grease and line the base of a 20 cm (8 inch) round cake tin with baking paper.

Put the dates in a saucepan with 250 ml (9 fl oz/1 cup) water. Cook, stirring occasionally, for 5–6 minutes until the dates are soft and the water has been absorbed. Remove from the heat and stir in the bicarbonate of soda and butter. Set aside for 10 minutes to cool slightly.

Transfer to a large mixing bowl, add the sugar, vanilla and eggs and stir well. Fold in the sifted flour until combined. Spoon into the tin and bake for 50 minutes, or until a skewer inserted into the centre comes out clean. Leave in the tin for 5 minutes, then turn out and cool on a wire rack. Serve with warm butterscotch sauce and ice cream.

BUTTERSCOTCH SAUCE

185 g (6½ oz/1 cup) soft brown sugar

200 ml (7 fl oz) cream

150 g (5½ oz) unsalted butter

Heat the sugar, cream and butter in a saucepan over a medium heat, stirring to dissolve the sugar. Bring to a simmer and cook over a low heat for 3 minutes. Pour over the sticky date cake to serve. Makes 500 ml (17 fl oz/2 cups).

cherry tart

pastry
125 g (4½ oz) unsalted butter, melted and cooled
90 g (3¼ oz) caster (superfine) sugar
175 g (6 oz) plain (all-purpose) flour
a pinch of salt
2 tablespoons ground almonds

filling
170 ml (5½ fl oz/⅔ cup) cream
2 eggs, lightly beaten
2 teaspoons natural vanilla extract
3 tablespoons caster (superfine) sugar
2 tablespoons plain (all-purpose) flour
550 g (1 lb 4 oz) cherries, halved and stoned (fresh are best)

to serve
cream or ice cream

Preheat the oven to 180°C (350°F/Gas 4) and grease a 24 cm (9½ inch) round loose-based tart tin. To make the pastry, stir together the butter and sugar in a large mixing bowl. Add the flour and salt and stir to make a soft dough. Transfer the dough to the tin and press evenly into the base and side of the tin with your fingertips. Put the tin on a baking tray and bake for 12–15 minutes, or until the pastry is slightly puffy. Remove from the oven and sprinkle the ground almonds over the base.

Meanwhile, to make the filling, whisk together the cream, eggs, vanilla and sugar. Add the flour and whisk until well mixed. Arrange the cherries, slightly overlapping, over the pastry base and pour the cream filling evenly over the cherries.

Return the tart to the oven for a further 40–50 minutes until the filling is firm. Leave to cool and serve with cream or ice cream.

coconut rice pudding with caramelised pineapple

SERVES 4

400 ml (14 fl oz) coconut milk
500 ml (17 fl oz/2 cups) milk
225 g (8 oz/1 cup) arborio rice
3 tablespoons caster (superfine) sugar
1 teaspoon natural vanilla extract

to serve
caramelised pineapple (see below)

Preheat the oven to 170°C (325°F/Gas 3) and lightly grease a 1.5 litre (52 fl oz/6 cup) baking dish.

Put the coconut milk, milk, rice, sugar and vanilla in the dish and stir together well. Cover with foil and bake for 1¼ hours, then remove the foil and return to the oven for another 30–35 minutes, until nicely browned on top. Leave to rest for 10 minutes before serving with caramelised pineapple.

CARAMELISED PINEAPPLE

½ teaspoon ground cinnamon
2 tablespoons soft brown sugar
3 thin slices fresh pineapple, cut into small triangles

Mix together the cinnamon and sugar on a large plate. Toss the pineapple triangles in the cinnamon sugar, so they are coated on all sides.

Heat a large non-stick frying pan over a medium-high heat and cook the pineapple for 1 minute on each side or until caramelised. Serve with the rice pudding.

baked lemon lime tart with fresh strawberry salad

SERVES 8 TO 10

4 eggs
170 g (6 oz/¾ cup) caster (superfine) sugar
125 ml (4 fll oz/½ cup) cream
80 ml (2½ fl oz/⅓ cup) lemon juice
80 ml (2½ fl oz/⅓ cup) lime juice
baked sweet shortcrust pastry shell
(see below) or ready-made shortcrust
pastry shell

to serve
250 g (9 oz/1⅔ cups) strawberries, hulled
and cut into quarters
1 tablespoon honey
1 tablespoon Cointreau (optional)
thick (double/heavy) cream (optional)

Preheat the oven to 160°C (315°F/Gas 2–3). Place the eggs and sugar in a bowl and whisk to combine. Add the cream then the lemon and lime juices and whisk lightly until just combined. Pour the mixture into the cooled pastry shell and bake for 25–30 minutes, or until just set. Remove from the oven and leave to cool. Place the strawberries, honey and Cointreau, if using, into a bowl and toss gently to combine. Leave to sit for 20 minutes. Serve with the tart and thick cream, if desired.

250 g (2 cups) plain (all-purpose) flour
125 g (4½ oz/1 cup) icing (confectioners')
sugar, sifted
a pinch of salt
180 g (6¼ oz) unsalted butter, chilled
and cubed
60 ml (2 fl oz/¼ cup) iced water

BAKED SWEET SHORTCRUST PASTRY SHELL

Place the flour, icing sugar and salt into a bowl and stir to combine. Using your fingertips, rub the butter through until the mixture resembles coarse breadcrumbs. Add the water and mix until the dough comes together in a ball. Shape into a round, wrap in plastic wrap and chill for 30 minutes. Roll out on a lightly floured surface until 3 mm (⅛ inch) thick. Press into a greased or non-stick 23 cm (9 inch) tart tin and prick the pastry with a fork. Chill for a further 30 minutes.

Preheat the oven to 200°C (400°F/Gas 6). Line the chilled pastry with baking paper and add baking weights or rice. Bake for 15 minutes, then remove the paper and weights. Bake for another 10 minutes, or until golden and crisp. Leave to cool.

312

Index

Published in 2011 by Murdoch Books Pty Limited

Murdoch Books Australia
Pier 8/9
23 Hickson Road
Millers Point NSW 2000
Phone: +61 (0) 2 8220 2000
Fax: +61 (0) 2 8220 2558
www.murdochbooks.com.au

Murdoch Books UK Limited
Erico House, 6th Floor
93–99 Upper Richmond Road
Putney, London SW15 2TG
Phone: +44 (0) 20 8785 5995
Fax: +44 (0) 20 8785 5985
www.murdochbooks.co.uk

Publisher: Kylie Walker
Designer: Jay Ryves, Future Classic
Photographers: Petrina Tinslay. Additional photography by Steve Brown (pp. 4, 6, 8, 15, 58, 86, 130, 139, 156, 157, 176, 181, 268, 276, 298).
Stylists: Michelle Noerianto, Rebecca Cohen, Kristen Anderson, Marcus Hay, Briget Palmer, Bill Granger and Kristine Duran-Thiessen
Food Editors: Jane Lawson, Chrissy Freer, Lulu Grimes, Jody Vassallo and Sonia Greig
Project Editor: Gabriella Sterio
Production: Renee Melbourne

National Library of Australia Cataloguing-in-Publication entry

Author: Granger, Bill, 1969-
Title: Best of Bill: the ultimate collection of Bill Granger's recipes/Bill Granger
ISBN: 978-1-74266-351-7 (hbk.)
Notes: Includes index.
Subjects: Cooking.
Dewey Number: 641.5

A catalogue record for this book is available from the British Library.

Printed in 2011 by 1010 Printing International Limited, China.

IMPORTANT: Those who might be at risk from the effects of salmonella poisoning (the elderly, pregnant women, young children and those suffering from immune deficiency diseases) should consult their doctor with any concerns about eating raw eggs.

OVEN GUIDE: You may find cooking times vary depending on the oven you are using. For fan-forced ovens, as a general rule, set the oven temperature to 20°C (35°F) lower than indicated in the recipe.